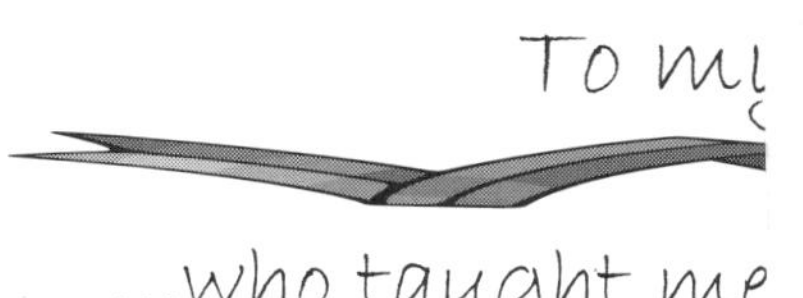

To my...
...who taught me
love with all my heart and
never stop learning.

But nobody said it had to be hard!
Certainly, learning how to use a computer doesn't have to be hard at all. With this little guide, you'll get the hang of Windows 7 in no time at all.

Live, Love, Learn

The sale of this book, and other books in the My Parents Computer book series, support the fight against cancer. Find a cure.

www.MyParentsFirst.com

Published by KLMK Enterprises, Delta, BC
www.MyParentsFirst.com

Printed by Hignell Printing, Winnipeg, MB, Canada
First Edition December 2010   ISBN 978-0-9732728-7-1

Back cover photo by Mark Doucette Photography,
St. Margaret's Bay, NS

i

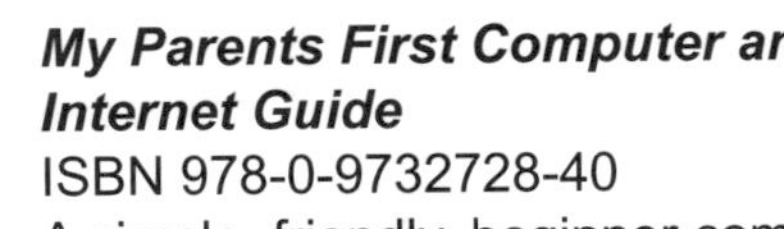
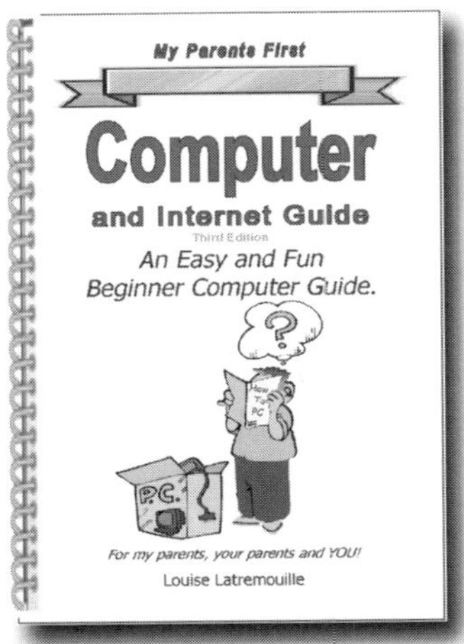

My Parents First Computer and Internet Guide
ISBN 978-0-9732728-40
A simple, friendly, beginner computer guide, written in plain everyday language. Follow easy, straight-forward steps to get comfortable with your computer.

Geared to Windows XP, introduces Vista.

Over 33,000 copies sold! Friends keep telling friends about this easy book...

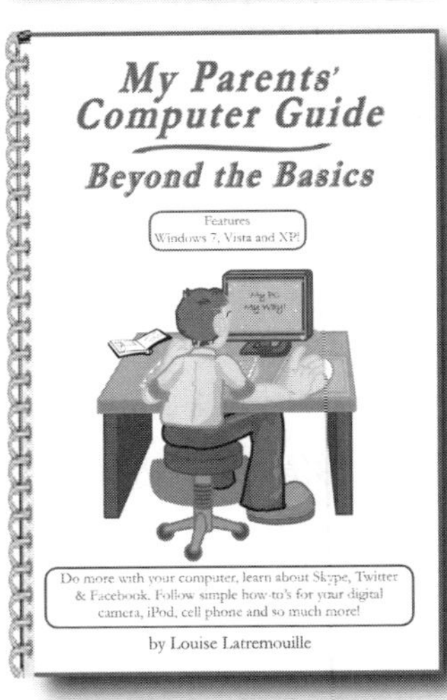

My Parents Computer and Internet Guide, Beyond the Basics
ISBN 978-0-9732728-64
Quick and simple. This is a companion book for *My Parents First...* or *My Parents Get Windows 7*. It's perfect for those who are ready to go *beyond the basics.* Get more out of Word classic and learn to use Excel. Learn about internet security, do online banking, use Facebook, Skype and Twitter. There's even simple how-to's for digital cameras, mp3 players, cell phones and more!
2010 Release.

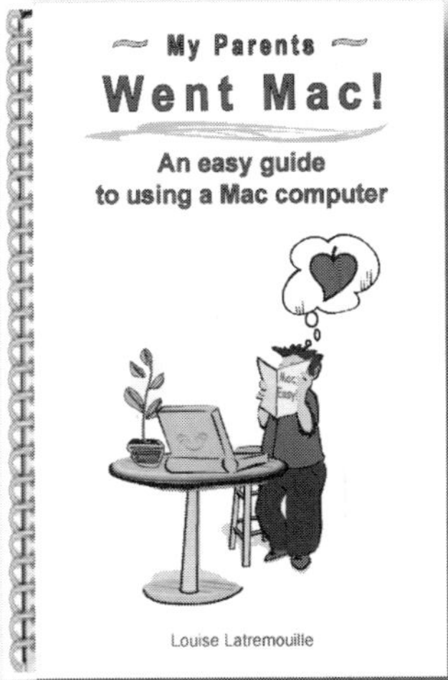

My Parents Went Mac!
ISBN 978-0-9732728-33
Finally, an easy beginner guide for Mac users! Follow the quick steps to personalize your Mac. Before you know it you will be on the internet with Safari and using Mail. Learn how to use iTunes and iPhoto too. Learning to use a Mac has never been so simple!

"This, is an easy read!"

OVER 6,500 copies sold!
2009 Release.

My Parents Get Windows 7

Welcome to Windows 7, this guide will get you up and going in no time at all. Just follow the easy steps.

Each quick chapter will give you the building blocks to go on to the next. Before you know it you'll be surfing the internet, using e-mail, making the most of your digital pictures and more!

"...It`s like a patient teacher, gently guiding you along."

Your Computer and You

Are you a PC or a Mac?
These are the two main types of computers that the general population uses. *PC* stands for Personal Computer and a *Mac* is a type of computer built by Apple.

Inside any computer is an operating system that sets the tone for how it will work. *Windows XP, Vista* and *Windows 7* are all *operating systems* for PCs.

Operating systems are like a conductor to an orchestra; they bring everything together to make beautiful music.

Windows 7 is a very nice conductor and this is going to be fun!

Ready? Let's go!

What's What?

Laptop or a Desktop?

They can have the same technology and abilities, so either/or, it's your choice.

Portability, is of course the biggest difference.
It's hard to pack a desktop into a briefcase...
Laptops have all their parts tucked in neatly together.

A computer desktop system includes:

The Tower
The tower holds all the parts that make your computer work; the motherboard, power supply, hard drives, disk drives, as well as all the ports that you use to plug your system together.

The Monitor is the computer screen.

The Keyboard is where you type.

The Mouse is used to quickly navigate on the monitor.

Speakers and a **printer** are also good items to include!

Buying a computer can be a little confusing...

A computer might grab your attention because it looks good, but after that, you`ll want to get to know it a little better.

Its beauty might grab you, but its brains will keep you!

What's in there?

Buying a Computer

Are you purchasing a computer?
There are a couple of things to consider...
Beauty and brains!

Beauty on the outside...

The Keyboard
Make sure the keyboard is comfortable for you to use. Do you want the number keypad that's on a regular keyboard? Number pads are not included on smaller keyboards.

The Monitor
LCD monitors are reliable, lightweight and use very little power. A high "refresh" rate can make watching videos the same as on your TV. A high pixel ratio means clearer, more vivid images. Make sure it comes with a fully adjustable stand, as the screen can look poor at odd angles. And, make sure the monitor is big enough for what you want.

Ports
Ports are like plug-ins. Everything you attach to your computer is connected via a port.

Each port is made for a specific device.
Different types of ports have different shapes, so you can't plug the wrong things together. *Nice!*

On a laptop, ports are usually on the sides.
On a desktop, most ports are found on the front and back of the tower. It's good to have USB ports on the front of a tower, so it's easy to connect things like an iPod or a camera.

USB Ports

Most electronic devices will connect to your computer via a USB port. USB stands for Universal Serial Bus. *Universal* being the key word! It's nice to have at <u>least</u> 3 or 4 USB ports on a computer.

Ethernet Port

An ethernet port is what you need to connect to a high speed internet cable. Even if the computer has built-in wireless internet, make sure there is an actual ethernet port too.

Dial-up Modem Port

When you use a telephone line to access the internet, it's referred to as dial-up. If that's your plan, you will need this type of port. It looks just like a regular telephone jack.

Monitor/Projector port

Connect the monitor to this port. If you have a laptop, you can connect a second monitor! It is also the kind of port you need if you want to connect a projector to your computer.

Firewire Port

Firewire is generally faster than USB wire and is often used to download videos from digital camcorders. If you have a camcorder that uses firewire you will need a firewire port. *Many camcorders use a USB connection.*

Headphone/Microphone Port

If you want to use headphones or a mic, look for audio-in and audio-out ports.

What You Want: Beauty

HDMI Port

If you think you might want to connect your computer to a High Definition TV, this is the type of port you want. It's a really nice way to view pictures and movies!

By the by..., You have to use a HDMI Cable with a HDMI Port. The cable must be compatible with TV and computer. Be sure to TURN OFF both your computer and TV while connecting. For viewing movies, if you want sound to come from your TV instead of your computer, open the control panel in your computer and change the sound setting:
Control Panel > Sound.

Optical Drive for CDs or DVDs

You need a disk drive to play CDs or DVDs. If the disk drive is also a **Burner**, you can copy pictures and files onto disks! *To play Blu-ray disks, you need a Blu-ray drive. Blu-ray uses a different technology.*

Web Cam

You need a web cam if you want to do video calls — like you can with Skype. Web cams are included with most laptops, and are also on many free standing monitors. You can also buy a separate web cam that plugs into a USB port.

A computer that is comfortable to use and easy to understand is a beautiful thing!
Want to make a couple notes?

Brains on the inside!

What you need is a quick processor, enough RAM to multi-task and plenty of hard drive to save things on.

Here's what I mean:

The Processor
CPU, Central Processing Unit

The CPU is your computer's main brain! It's where binary data is turned into normal looking stuff, like letters and pictures.

On average, computers come with about 2 GHz (gigahertz) of processing speed, fast enough for most users. Older processors were measured in MHz, (megahertz). Mega is million, Giga is billion cycles per second — way faster!

Having a "Duel Core" processor is a good thing. Information comes to and from the processor via a "core", having a duel core doubles how fast your computer can think. Quad core... *Now that'll be FAST!*

What do those dreaded acronyms mean?	
Speed	
MHz	Megahertz - a million cycles per second
GHz	Gigahertz - a billion cycles per second
Size	
MB	Megabyte - about 1 millions bytes of memory
GB	Gigabyte - about 1,000 Megabytes
TB	Terabyte - about 1 Trillion bytes, or 1,000 GB

What You Need: Brains

RAM

RAM stands for Random Access Memory, and is your computer's temporary, short term, working memory. It's the place where your computer can show off multi-tasking!

Until you save a file on your hard drive, your computer will use RAM space to hold your work on. Programs also need RAM space when they are being used.

How much RAM do you need? *Size can mean speed...*
1 GB will get you by if you're not using any large programs. 2 GB is better, but with 4 GB your computer will keep up with you. 6 GB is more than most need!

Hard Drive

This is where all your programs and files are stored. The bigger the hard drive, the more information your computer can hold.

Hard Drive Size?

Many computers only have a 250 GB (Gigabyte) hard drive. In new computers you might see 1 TB (Terabyte) hard drive. *Holy cow, now that's a huge hard drive!* A 500 GB hard drive is more than enough for most users.

Hard Drive Speed?

Hard drives have wafer thin disks that spin like a CD in a CD player. The disk spins and data is written onto it. The faster it spins, the faster it can write. 5400 RPMs or 7200 RPMs is pretty standard. *I don't find a difference using either one.*

But, it takes more power to run at 7200. So, if you've got a laptop and want to go unplugged for hours the battery will wear down faster at 7200 than it would at 5400.

Beauty and Brains: Parts Chart

BEAUTY	
Keyboard	Make sure it is comfortable to use.
Monitor	Make sure it has a good refresh rate and has an adjustable stand.
USB Ports	You'll want at least 4 USB Ports.
Ethernet Port (tech name RJ-45)	You need this for a high-speed internet cable.
Phone Port	Needed for a dial-up internet connection.
HDMI Port	Needed to hook up to a high-def TV
Firewire Port	Some digital camcorders use firewire instead of USB cord to transfer data.
CD/DVD Drive with Burner?	You need a CD/DVD drive. It's a good option if it's a Burner too.
Wi-Fi	You might want it to have built in wireless internet capability.

BRAINS	**Basic needs**	**What's it for**
Processor, CPU	1 GHz, minimum 2 GHz, average 4 GHz, fast	The brain of your computer. GHz is about speed.
Memory, RAM	1 GB, slow 2 GB, better 4 GB, fast.	The working area of your computer. GB is about size.
Hard Drive, HD	250 GB, minimum 500 GB, average 750 GB, large 1 TB, extra large!	What your files, pictures and programs are stored on.
Graphics card	A better graphics/video card will let you see sharper images and videos.	
Sound/Audio Card	You need a sound card for speakers or a microphone to work.	

Bright Ideas

Want to write down some notes?

Get Turned On

Computers are pretty snazzy and are
becoming more and more
user friendly every day.
Keyboards are more comfortable and
screens are easier on the eyes.
Besides helping you keep in touch with
friends and family, they can be fun and
make your life easier.

Get Turned On

Let's Turn You On — and Off!

 Somewhere on your computer is a power button. **Turn it on** and let`s get started!

When you turn on a computer it goes through its startup sequence. You`ll hear whirring and a few beeps. Don't push any buttons until it's finished starting up; it doesn't take long. Click on *Welcome* when your computer settles down to open your desktop.

Here's how to shut down:

Click on the Start button, then move your mouse up and over to Shut down. **Click on the little arrow to see your options.**
Start > Shut Down > ...

The options can help you save money and power!

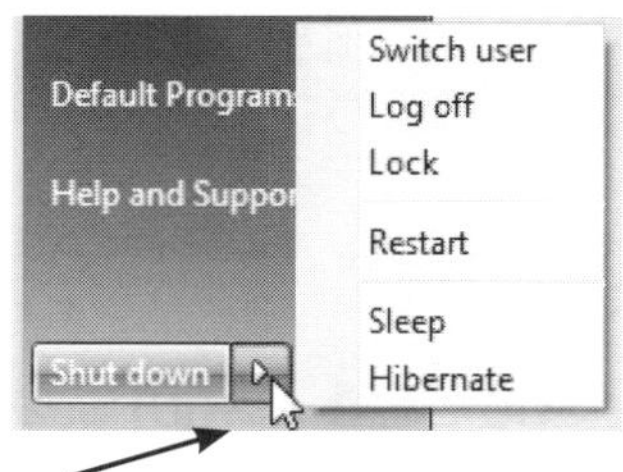

If you have a laptop, using Sleep and Hibernate will help the battery last longer. If you are using a desktop, using these settings can help you save big time on your power bill!

♦ **Sleep** is just like pausing a movie. Everything seems to shut down, but is ready to go again with a single touch.

♦ **Hibernate** shuts down your computer but leaves all the programs you have going open. Everything will be there, ready to work with when you restart.

Shut down
Closes any programs you have open and turns off your computer!

The Keyboard

Most of the keys are just like a regular typewriter, but some are specifically for a computer.

This is a standard, full-size keyboard that includes a number pad on the right. Press the "num lock" key to use the number pad like a calculator.

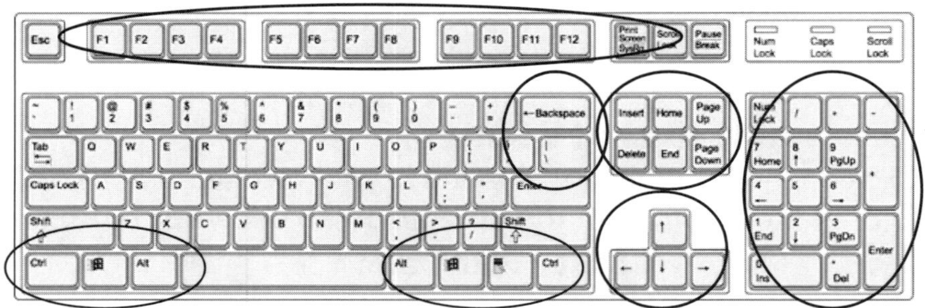

CTRL key

This is the Control key. Press it together with another key to create a command shortcut. For instance, press CTRL and "C" together for copy. CTRL and "V", for paste.

Windows key 

Press the Windows key and you will open the Start menu!

Alt key

The Alt key is like a second CTRL key. Depending on the program, you can use it as a keyboard shortcut for some commands.

Here's something fun with the Alt key...

Using a font like Arial (this typing is in the font Arial) or Times New Roman and using the number pad, press:

the Alt key & 1 to make ☺ *or,* the Alt key & 3 to make 

Function keys

Along the top of your keyboard you will see the F-keys: F1 to F12. What they do can be different from program to program and sometimes they do nothing at all!

But... F1 is usually a shortcut to Help!

FN key

If your F keys have little pictures (icons) on them, you will have an FN key. It's usually located beside the CRTL key.

The fn key works like this:

Say your F3 key also has a ▶ (speaker) icon on it. Press the FN key + F3 together to change the volume on your computer! *The features vary from keyboard to keyboard.*

Try them out on yours!

Backspace & Delete keys

Click on Backspace and you will erase typing to the left.
Click on the Delete key and you'll erase typing to the right!

Insert key

The Insert key is an important key to know. Activate the Insert key and you'll be inserting type. Deactivate it and you'll type over and replace what you've already typed.

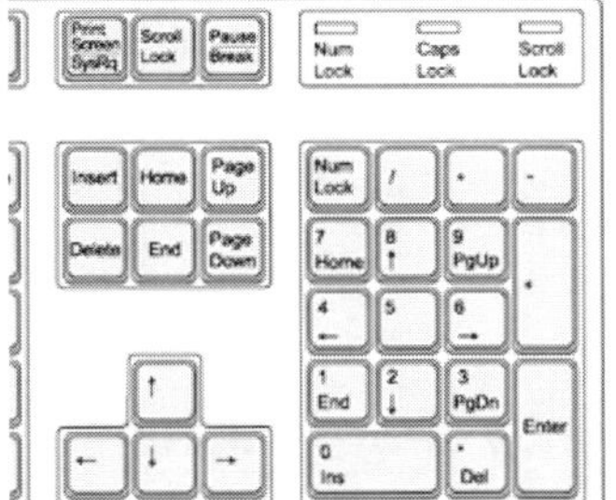

Arrow keys

Use these to move your cursor up, down, left or right on your screen.

Mouse in the House

The computer mouse has made it possible for everyone to feel like a pro! Here's how:

On your monitor...

When you move your mouse, you will see an arrow, *or cursor,* move around on your screen. They will move together, like good dance partners!

Left-click, Right-click

The top of your mouse has two buttons; the left and right clicks.

Right-click to get commands.

Right-click your mouse and you will open up a mouse menu full of commands. If you right-click when using Word, you will see a menu with options like copy, cut, font... If you right-click on an empty space on your desktop, you will get a menu to personalize your desktop. The menu will change to suit where you are using your mouse!

Greyed out commands aren't available. For instance, you can't Paste, until you Copy!

Right-click again to give a command.

Right-click and choose a command, right-click again to see the options to finish the job.

Cut
Copy
Paste
Font
Paragraph

Left-click to point, select and highlight.

Left-click your mouse anywhere on your screen and the cursor will land there. Ready for you to type!

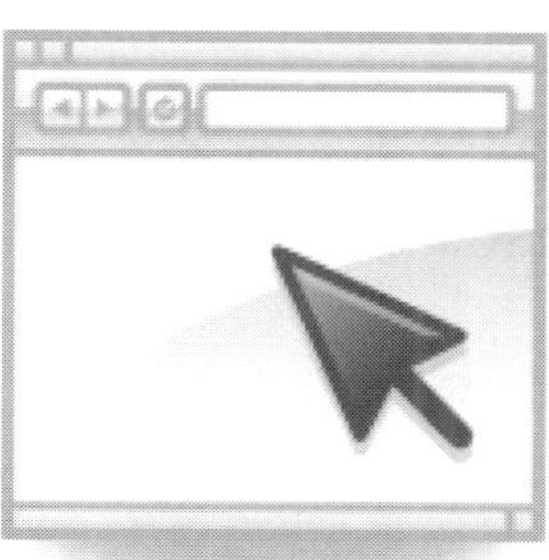

Here's how to highlight!

Holding the left-click down, drag your mouse over text. It will highlight as you drag. **This is a great way to copy/paste. Here's how:**

1. Highlight text
2. Right-click, choose Copy (the highlighting will go away)
3. Left-click your mouse where you want to paste the text
4. Right-click again, choose Paste

A Roller

A computer mouse might also have a roller. If you have one, try it out! With it you can scroll up and down pages on your screen. It's a great feature.

YOU CAN CUSTOMIZE YOUR MOUSE...

If you are left-handed,
you might want to change what the left and right-clicks do.
Click through this path to see all the mouse options:
Start > Control Panel > Mouse

BUT, IN THIS BOOK...
RIGHT-CLICK GETS COMMANDS.

The Start Menu

The Start menu is the grand entrance to your computer. From here you can open any program or file.

The left side column will show a list of your most recently used programs. A nice shortcut to open them again!

The right side column always stays the same, showing important folders in your computer.

When you click on **All Programs**, you'll open a menu showing all the programs installed in your computer.
You might have to slide a *scroll bar* that could show up beside the list to see everything.
Click on a program's name to open it.

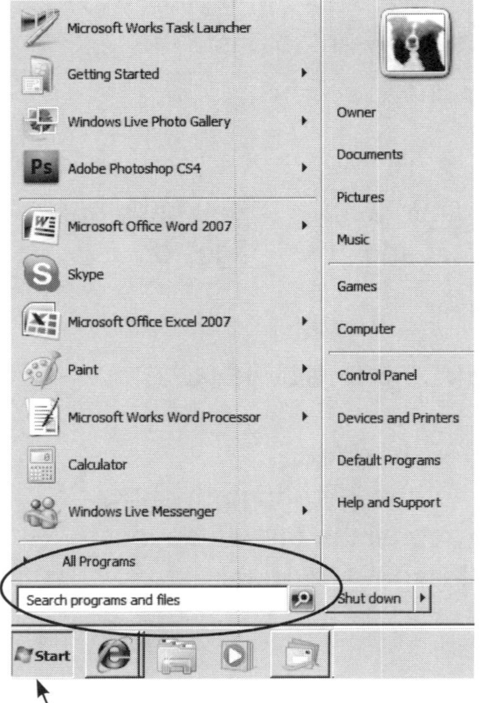

The Search window is the BEST in Windows 7! See it just above the Start button?

To find a program or file, start typing the name of the file or program you're looking for in the search box. Instantly, results will start to show up in the column right above it.

When what you're looking for shows up, left-click on the file or program to open it.

The Start menu button is down in the left corner.

The Taskbar

The taskbar shows an icon for any program that's open and it's a great place to dock shortcuts!
The Start button sits on the left side of the taskbar.

The Taskbar has some very cool features.

1. **Shortcuts.** Open a program instantly by clicking on its icon along the taskbar.

2. **Jump Lists.** Right-click on an icon and you will see a menu of all the last files you had open with that program. Just slide your mouse up and click on the file you want.

3. **Thumbnails.** An icon will show on the taskbar for each program you have open. Hover your mouse over a program's icon to see a thumbnail view of all the pages that program currently has open. *Try it out, it's very cool!*

4. **Pinning**. Pin a program to the taskbar and the icon will stay there as a shortcut to open the program.
   Here's how:

   1. Find the program you want: Start > All Programs. Search for the program you want.

   2. **Right-click** over a program`s name and choose "Pin to taskbar".

   Want something un-pinned?
   Right-click on the icon and choose "Unpin this program from taskbar". *Can't get any easier than that!*

The Personal Touch

Personalize your desktop. You can personalize what your computer screen looks like when your computer is idle.

You can change the background picture on your desktop, pick out sounds, choose a screen saver... **Here's how:**

1. Right-click anywhere on your desktop to open a mouse menu.

2. Then, click on *Personalize* to open the window that shows all your options.

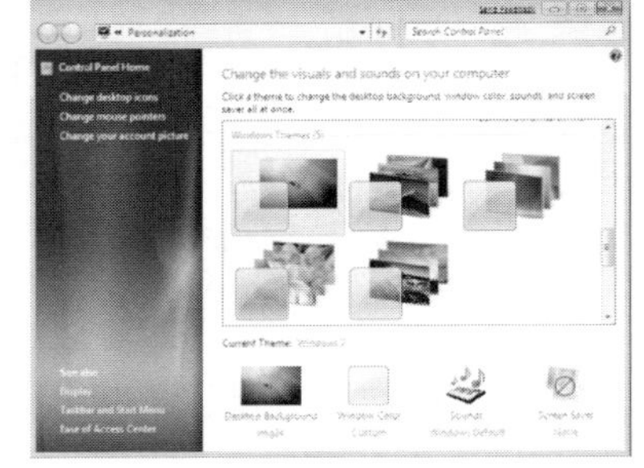

3. Pick and choose the options to create your favorite look!

You can't mess things up here so go ahead, get creative.

Try things out for fun!

Your desktop background can even be a slide show of your favorite pictures! **Here's how:**

1. Under "Aero Themes" click on Windows 7.

2. *Then* click on "Desktop Background" *on the bottom of this screen.*

3. In the next window that opens, click on "Browse" to find the folder that your pictures are saved in. Should be "Libraries > Pictures". Click OK.

4. You can pick and choose the pictures by ticking on any you want to be included and unticking any you don't.

5. Save and Close when you're done. *WooHoo!*

You might want to make a favorite picture your desktop background. There's a few of ways to do that:

♦ From the internet.
Maybe you're are surfing the net and see a picture you love. Right-click your mouse over the picture to open a mouse menu that includes, "Set as background". Left-click over the command and instantly, it's your background. Ta Da!

FYI... Some pictures are very low resolution and look blurry when they are stretched out on your desktop.

♦ From pictures you've saved in your computer.

Here's how to open your Pictures folder:

1. Open *Windows Explorer* by clicking on its icon on the taskbar.
2. In the left column, under *Libraries,* click on *Pictures.*
3. You might have many folders (albums) of pictures. Click on a folder to open it. When you see the picture you want, right-click over it to see the option "Set it as your desktop background". Left-click on the command tand you've done it!

♦ From an e-mailed picture.
Click on the picture or attachment to open it. Right-click over the picture to see either the options to save the picture or set it as your background.

Making a Backup!

Backing up your computer with Windows 7 is SOOOO easy that I am including it right here. *For future reference!*

What is a Backup?

It is a copy of the data in your computer, like pictures, documents, programs...

Why Backup?

Because stuff happens... "My computer crashed, I lost everything". If you keep a current backup, that won't happen to you. A sick computer can be just an inconvenience, not a disaster.

Backup Where?

Here are some options:

♦ Onto a USB Memory stick . A four or eight GB memory stick is often big enough. Memory sticks are usually around $20.

♦ Onto a re-writable DVD, if your DVD drive is a Burner.

♦ Onto a separate hard drive unit; these can cost $70 plus.

Making a Backup!

Here's how:
Click your mouse through this path:

> Start > Control Panel > System and Maintenance >
> Backup and Restore

OR

Type "backup" in the Search window. When you see
"Backup and Restore" in the space above, click on it!

Before you go on to the next step...
Attach or insert whatever you are going to put the backup on.

If this is the first time you are doing a backup, click on
Set up Backup and follow the Wizard!

If you want to change where you did a previous backup...

♦ Click on Options, near the top of the Backup window.
♦ Click on Change, or Change Settings
♦ In the "options" window, choose where you want to backup

*You can let Windows choose what to backup (a good idea)
or you can pick and choose what you want. Make sure you
backup the "C" drive though, as it's your main hard drive.*

*Knowing you have a
backup plan can take
your worries away!*

Those Top Three Boxes

Before we get on any further, we need to quickly cover these **top three boxes!**

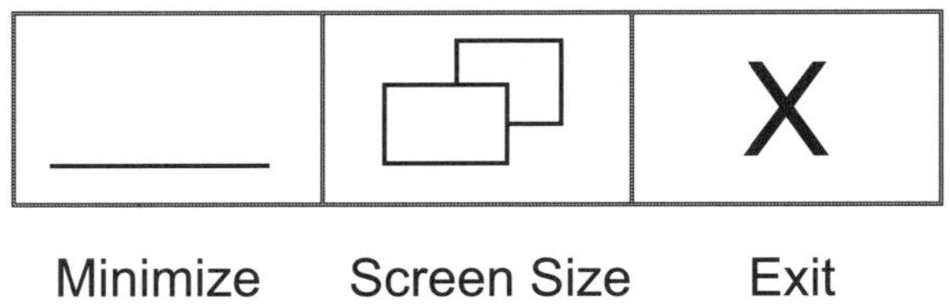

Minimize   Screen Size   Exit

You will see these three boxes on the top right-hand corner on almost any window. **Here's what they do:**

Minimize
Click on minimize to shrink the window you have open into the taskbar.

Screen Size View
Click on the middle box to change the size of the window you are viewing to either full-screen or partial-screen size.

Exit
Click on the "X" to close the program, window or document you have open. On a nice note, most programs will ask if you want to save the changes to a document you are working on before you close it.

Ready for more?
Good. Let's go!

Want to write down some notes? ______________________

Bright Ideas

Want to write down some notes?

The Internet

The internet is an incredible thing.

It carries a wealth of information
and has changed the way
the world communicates forever.

Windows 7 is very internet savvy,
and soon, you will be too!

The Internet

E-mail, live video calls, searching the internet for ...*anything!*
The internet is pretty cool!
And often, the main reason to have a computer.

Wi-Fi?

I mention Wi-Fi now to point out that you don't ALWAYS have to pay to access the internet. *That is, if you have a laptop with wireless capability...*

When you see a sign that says **"Free Wi-Fi"** it means you can connect to a wireless internet network for free there. Many libraries and cafés offer free Wi-Fi.

Technically, Wi-Fi is a Wireless Local Area Network or WLAN.

Here's what's what, on setting up the internet at home.

There are three ways to connect to the internet:

1. With wireless technology.

2. With an ethernet cable that's connected from a high speed modem to your computer.

3. Via a phone line that's connected to an internet server. This is called "dial-up". It is a very slow connection.

Internet Service Provider (ISP)

The name says it all. This is the company that provides your home with an internet connection. Most telephone or cable companies offer internet service.

How much it costs can really vary, from as little as $20 to over $200 a month! Call around to find your best deal for what you need and want. There are hook up fees and then a monthly bill.

Getting the Internet

How the set-up works.

Many internet service providers (ISPs) will come to your home and install a modem, some just send instructions. Inside a modem is the technology that turns computer data into the kind of data that can travel along telephone or cable lines to move on the internet.

The modem is configured to communicate with your ISP's server. From the server your information can go anywhere!

If you set up a wireless network in your home, you still need a modem. A wireless router needs to connect to a modem.

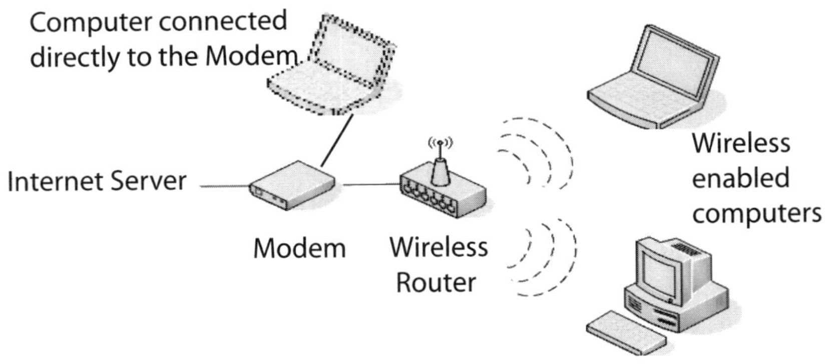

Your ISP will give you the information you'll need to set up e-mail accounts with them. Here's what's what:

♦ Your server's **name.**

♦ You'll create a **password** and your own **username.**

♦ Their **POP3** or **IMAP** setting for **incoming e-mail. (P**ost **O**ffice **P**rotocol or **I**nternet **M**essage **A**ccess **P**rotocol)

♦ The **SMTP** setting for **outgoing e-mail.**
(**S**imple **M**ail **T**ranser **P**rotocol)

Info from Your ISP

It's a good idea to write down some of the information your ISP will give you.

Your Username ___________________________________

The name your server knows you as, often your e-mail address

Your Password ___________________________________

Passwords should be confidential!
Maybe just write down a hint here!

Your e-mail address ___________________________________

POP or POP3 ___________________________________

pop.NameOfYourServer.com

IMAP ___________________________________

Your server will use either a POP account or IMAP, not both.

SMTP ___________________________________

smtp.NameOfYourServer.com

Your ISP's name ___________________________________

Your ISP's Help phone # ___________________________________

Your type of internet connection ___________________________________

Your internet connection password, or just a hint! _______

____

____

____

Internet Browsers

Is your computer already connected to the internet? Click on your internet browser and see if something is there!

Microsoft's browser is called Internet Explorer. You might see an icon for Internet Explorer in your taskbar. There are lots of other internet browsers out there, among them; Safari, Firefox, Opera, Google Chrome... You can use any browser you want; but in this book I'm sticking with Explorer.

Here's how to set up an internet connection: It's easy with the help of a wizard. Wizards walk you through things one step at a time!

1. Left-click through this path to open the Internet Wizard:
    Start > **Control Panel** > **Network and Internet** >
    Network and Sharing Center >

2. *Then, down on the bottom half of that screen, click on:*
    "Set up a connection or network"

3. *Finally... Choose Connect to the Internet.*   Ta da!

A wizard will now walk you through the next steps. All you have to do is type in the information you got from your service provider, in the spaces where it asks for it.

Click on *Next* at the bottom of each window, to go on to the next step. The last window will say *Finish. When you click on Finish you're connected!*

About Web Addresses

A website address is also known as a **Uniform Resource Locator or, *URL*.** *A common crossword clue!*

There are three parts to a web address.

1. **The prefix**, is *the part before www*. It tells your server what type of protocol the site uses. Protocols are the common rules that all of the internet must work with.

   Http:// is the prefix you will see for most websites. **Https://**, is for an encrypted, secure site. And **ftp://** is for transferring data to websites. Ftp stands for File Transfer Protocol.

2. **The domain name** is its title. People often only say this part of the address, omitting the prefix. That's okay, because your browser can figure the prefix out for itself.

3. **The *suffix*.** The suffix gives you an idea of what type of website it is. For example:

.com	Commercial Business
.ca	Canada
.edu	Educational Institution
.gov	Government Agency
.mil	Military
.net	Network Organization
.org	Organization (non-profit)

A typical web address might look like this:

http://www.nameofthesite.com

About Web Addresses

Every website has a home page, it's like a cover to a book. A small website might only have a home page.

When you look at a web address, the three parts in the beginning are a *website's home page.* These parts are always separated by periods, referred to as "*dot*".

Slashes at the end of an address indicate **links**, or if you like, other pages within that website.

http://www.nameofthesite.com/trees/flowers/contact/

You might see LOTS of slashes and links at the end of an address. The larger the site, the more links (pages within pages) there will be.

Often a large site will have its' own search tool to help people find what they are looking for.

For example, microsoft.com is a hugeomungazoid site. To find anything there, you really need to use their search tool.

Look for a search window, usually near the top of a page, and type in what you are looking for.

Bright Ideas

Want to write down some notes?

Internet Explorer

Internet Explorer is Microsoft's browser. The layout and some of the terms in other browsers might be a little different. For example, Favorites is called "Bookmarks" in Firefox.

Here's what's what on Internet Explorer.
Look for the corresponding # on the picture.

1. The website's title.

2. Back and Forward buttons.

3. Web Address window.

4. Refresh. Your computer remembers websites. Use refresh to upload the most current version of the website.

5. Click on the X to stop loading a page.

6. Search window. I show Google, but you can use another.

7. The Menu bar.

8. "Favorites" is an option I like, find it under View > Toolbars.

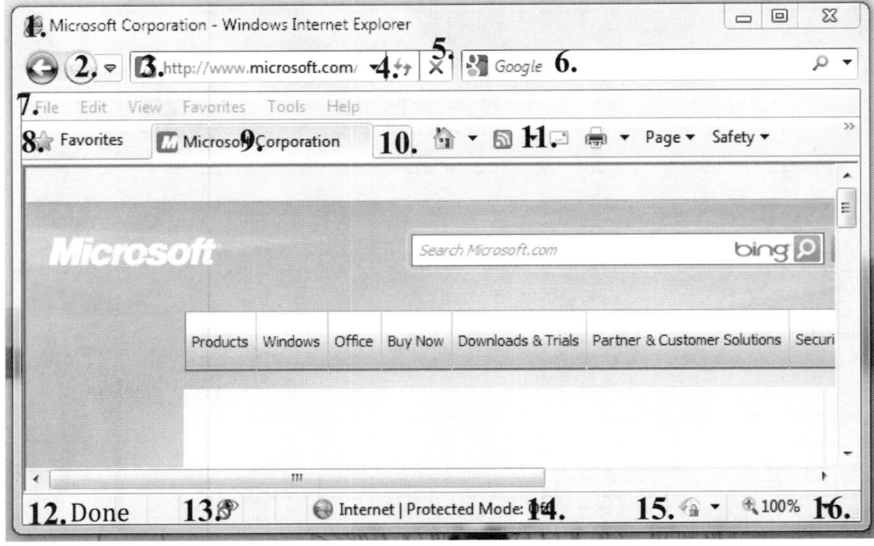

9. Tabs show the title of the webpage you're on.

10. Click on this Tab to open another website. You can click on the tabs to go back and forth between websites!

11. Icons: Home page, Feeds, E-mail and Print

12. This says *"Done"* now, but as a page is loading you'll see a green bar grow. Be patient! Look here if a webpage seems to be taking a long time to load and you will see what's happening.

13. Some websites will show this "Privacy Report". It has to do with what security settings you have set.

14. Internet Protection. To find *Set Your Security Settings*, Click through this path from the menu bar: Tools > Internet Options. Then, click on the Security tab. Adjust the slider to choose your own level of security.

15. This little lock will be colored if you are on a secure, encrypted site, like it should be if you're using your credit card on-line. It's greyed out if you are on a regular, non-encrypted site.

16. 100% - Click here to zoom in or out on a website. You can also press Ctrl and the **+** sign to zoom in, or **-** to zoom out.

Bookmark Your Favorites

Bookmark favorite websites.
With Internet Explorer, click on **Favorites** to save web
addresses on a handy list.

After you bookmark a website you can click on Favorites to
see the site listed. Click on it in the list, and —
Zoom, you're there!

You can even organize your favorite websites into their own
categories. Put a medical site into a folder named Health, or
your favorite team into Sports, etc.

If you don't file a website into a folder, it'll just go to the
bottom of your Favorites list.

Here's how:

*You must be on a website
to bookmark it.*

1. Move your mouse to the menu bar and left-click on
   Favorites.

2. In the window that opens, you'll see a text box with
   the website's name in it. You can change the name to
   anything you like, *the name is for your own reference.*

3. Choose where you want to file the bookmark. Either with
   your other *Favorites*, or filed into one of your *Favorites*
   folders. Click on *New Folder* if you want to make a new
   folder to file this website in.

4. When you're done, click *Add!*

Searching the Internet

The **World Wide Web** is a big big place and searching for things can be overwhelming.

Luckily, search engines, like Google and Bing, have made searching — *and finding!* — easy.

You don't really have to know how search engines work. But, knowing what they are looking for can make searching easier.

Here's a little of what's what...

♦ **Search Engines** are dedicated servers with programs that send out *spiders* (also called web crawlers).

♦ **Spiders** look for *keywords* that are embedded in web pages.

♦ **Keywords** are words that describe what's in a website. You often don't see keywords when you view a site. They are part of the *HTML* that is hidden on the viewing page, as they are only meant to help search engines find the site.

♦ **HTML** Hyper Text Markup Language is the computer language that most websites are written in.

Google.com, Bing.com, Yahoo.com, Ask.com
are all search engine sites.
There are more, but these are in the top 10.

Let's do a Google search on the next page for practice!

To practice, let's do a Google search.

Here's how:

- **Open your browser** and click your mouse in the address bar. *If you click your mouse at the very beginning of the address bar, the old address will erase when you begin typing!* **Type:**

www.google.com

1. On Google's home page, you will see a text box where you can type in what you are looking for. Type in the word ***vacation***, then click on Search.

- A ton of results will show up; there could be thousands. To narrow down your search, search again, but be more specific. Maybe you want to holiday in Nova Scotia, Canada.

2. Click back into the search box and type: ***vacation Nova Scotia Canada***

- Search engine *spiders* try to match up your words with website *keywords*. Then they show you all the results they found. You can even be more specific! Maybe you are searching for a hotel?

3. Click back into the search box and type: ***vacation Nova Scotia Canada hotel***

See the pattern?
The more *keywords* that you can think of, the better. Your search engine will do the work. From the resulting list, click on the website you want to look at!

◊ In the list of search results, look at the title, as well as the website address. Sometimes the title can be misleading.

◊ Use the back and forward buttons on your web browser's toolbar to go back to previous web pages. They are great tools if you landed on the wrong website.

Tip - Use "Quotation Marks"

If you do a search for Nova Scotia, you will get hits for just the word "Nova" too. Great if you want to learn about a super PBS show or outer space, but if you plan on staying on earth...

With "quotation marks" search engines will only look for the words together. "Nova Scotia". Smart cookies!

Social Media, You're Responsible

"For more information, have a look at our website", is a line you hear often these days. You'll hear it on the news, on the radio, see it on commercials... It is part of today's culture.

Social media sites, such as Facebook, Twitter and YouTube, are a huge part of today's culture too. Face it, if you are not on Facebook, you know someone who is.

You might not want to join these groups, but if you have kids or grandkids who are using these sites, you should learn how to use them too.

We need to teach our children how to be safe in this cyber-world of ours. *Be "friends" with your kids on Facebook.*

♦ Let them be proud and feel good about their friends.

♦ Guide them in social responsibility.

♦ Teach them about cyber-bullying.

♦ Teach them how to set privacy settings on social media sites, and the reasons why these settings are important.

♦ Talk to them about pictures they might post. What's appropriate, what's not.

All about Facebook, Twitter and Skype is in the next book in this series: <u>My Parents' Computer Guide, Beyond the Basics</u>.

When you're finished this book, you *will* feel comfortable on your computer and be ready to go beyond the basics. Really!

Nothing's hard to learn. Trust me. ☺

Essentially E-Mail

You`ve Got Mail.
E-mail that you can access
from anywhere in the world!

Not only can you e-mail, but you can also
blog, share photos, instant message,
make movies and so much more.
Windows Live Essentials
has a lot going for it!

Essentially E-Mail

Now that you've learned how to get on the internet, you're ready to learn about Windows Live Mail.

> *Windows Live Mail replaces Outlook Express and Windows Mail that was included with Vista and XP.*

Unlike previous operating systems, with Windows 7 you have to download and install Microsoft's newest e-mail program.

Don't freak out
at the idea of downloading a
program so early in the game.
It's super easy to do, because
your computer knows where to put
things and what to do with them!

Before we get going with Windows Live Mail,
I thought we should quickly go over
what makes up an e-mail address.

There are three parts to an e-mail address.

1. The name.

2. The "@" sign; found above the number 2 on your keyboard. *Use the shift key to get to it.*

3. The server or domain name of where it is sent to.

A typical e-mail address looks like this:
YourName@YourServer.com

There are never spaces in an e-mail address.
When someone says "dot" they mean a period.

Live Essentials

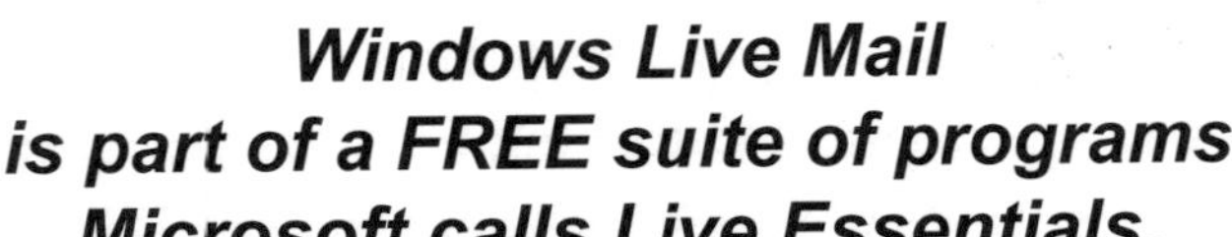

Windows Live Mail
is part of a FREE suite of programs
Microsoft calls Live Essentials.

You can download all of the programs or just the ones you want. I recommend downloading everything because the programs work so well together.

Here's what's what:

◆   **Mail** - For e-mail.

◆   **Photo Gallery** - Create albums, edit and share pictures.

◆   **Messenger** - Chat or make live video calls.

◆   **Movie Maker** - For making and editing movies for the web and creating great slide shows.

◆   **Writer** - All set up to create and publish blogs (blogs are a web diary).

◆   **Family Safety** - Censor what websites your kids surf.

On the next few pages we'll walk through
the simple download and easy set up. No worries.

Download Windows Live Mail

Here's how:

1. Click on the Start button (Windows icon)

2. Slide your mouse up to Getting Started

3. Then, slide it over and click on Get Windows Live Essentials

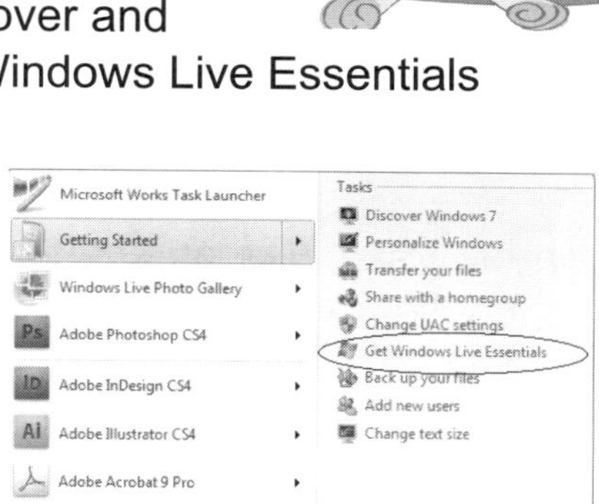

You will instantly go to the Windows Live Essentials website.

http://explore.live.com

- *Click on the big "Download Now" button. Notice that you have a choice of languages!*

- Next you'll see, "You have chosen to download "wlsetupweb.exe" *That's the name of the Windows Live set up program.*

- Click on SAVE! *It's a really fast download.*

- Once it's downloaded, click RUN.

Download Windows Live Mail

When you click on Run, a new "Welcome" window opens.
This wizard will walk you through the steps to do the install.

Read what the windows say, pick and choose what programs
you want to install, and keep clicking "next" until you're
finished. *It's really that easy.* Here's a bit of what's what...

♦ Put a tick mark beside the program(s) you want to install.
Untick anything you don't want installed.

   ♦ **Please install Mail!**

   ♦ I also recommend you **install Photo Gallery**, we'll
   be learning that next! ***And Movie Maker**, because
   you can use it with Photo Gallery....* Look at the other
   programs, tick the ones you want. ***Maybe all of them!!***

♦ *Then... Click on Install.*

♦ Let it do ALL the hard work. Things will go where they are
suppose to go and it will do what it's suppose to do. All
you have to do is read the windows that pop up. Pick and
choose the options you want.

Windows Live ID

Before the setup is done, it will ask you if you have a **Windows Live ID.**

A Windows Live ID is a Microsoft e-mail address, like;

you@live.ca   *or*   you@hotmail.com

If you already use Hotmail, Messenger or even X-box Live, your sign-in with those can be your Windows Live ID. If you don't have one, **click on SIGN UP**. Then:

♦ Fill in all the spaces on the small form.

♦ The next step helps prevent spam. By typing in the squiggly letters (you will see shown in a box), you tell their system you are a real person doing this.

♦ Click on "I accept".

Now, it will finish going through its installation process...
If it asks, click on Run to finish the install.

After all the programs you want are all installed, find them through your Start Menu in the Windows Live folder.

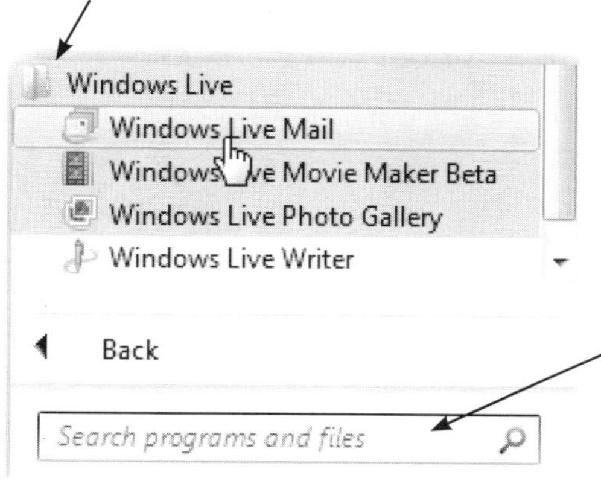

Type: *Windows Live* *in the "Search" box and you will see the Windows Live folder appear in the menu above it!*
Click on the folder to see the programs inside.

Make a Shortcut!

These are shortcuts you can make from the Start Menu.	♦ Pin to Taskbar ♦ Pin to Start Menu ♦ Send to > Desktop (create shortcut)

How to create a shortcut.

1. Click on the Start button, then *All Programs. Or, type the name of a program in the Search window!*

2. **Right-click** on the program you want to make a shortcut for.
   You will open a mouse menu with shortcut options!

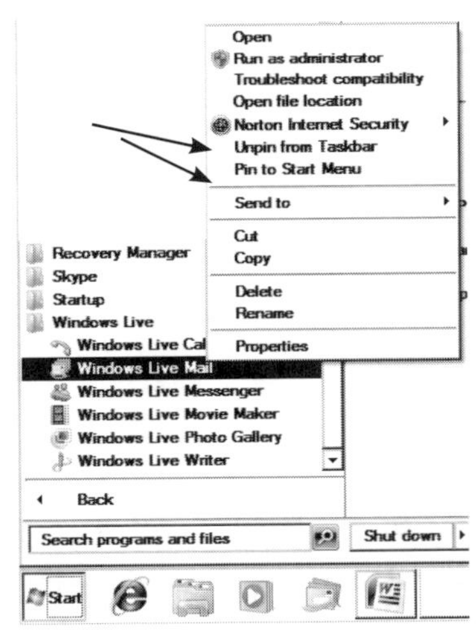

3. Move your mouse up to the shortcut you want and left-click on it.

Want to write down some notes?

Open Mail

Open Mail!

Click on the shortcut you just created.
or
Open Mail through the Start Menu.

Live Mail has a nice clean layout and the tools you need are easy to find. I'll show you what's what on the next few pages.

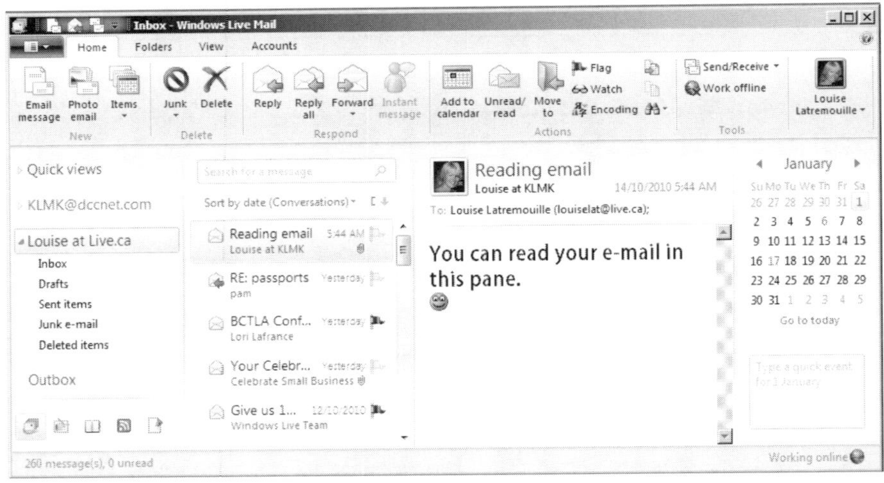

One of the nice features of Live Mail is that *if* you have a variety of e-mail address, you can view them all here. You might not think it, but it's pretty easy to get more than one e-mail address. Maybe you have one from work, one with your local internet provider and a Hotmail address. Under each e-mail account name, you'll see a group of folders that hold all that account's e-mail.

Let's go over what these folders are for. Can you see them in the left side column? The Inbox, Drafts, Sent items, Junk e-mail, Deleted items and Outbox folders.

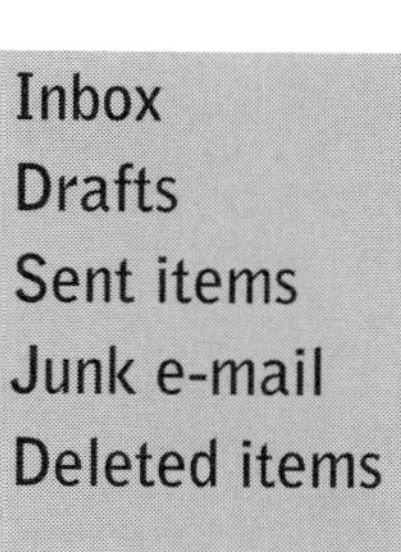

Inbox
When you receive e-mail, it'll go into this folder.

Drafts
If you start an e-mail but don't send it, you can save it in your Drafts folder.
To send an e-mail to the Drafts folder click on the "X", as if you were going to close it. A little window will open asking if you want to save it in your Drafts folder or Delete it. Choose, *Save it in your Drafts folder.*

Sent items
You got it, this folder keeps a copy of all the e-mails you send.

Junk e-mail
Live Mail will think some e-mail is junk and file it here. The funny thing about the Junk folder is that you can't *preview* e-mails that land here without opening them, a feature that's part of all the other folders. *In my opinion, this is not a good thing. Of all the folders, this is the one that will have e-mail you might not want to open. But what the heck, it is what it is.*

Deleted items
When you delete e-mail, they go to this folder. It's important to empty your Deleted items folder regularly to help keep your system running without clutter. Just right-click over "Deleted items" and you'll see the option to Empty it.

Outbox
After you hit "send" on an e-mail you've written, while Mail is actually sending it, you will see it momentarily in your Outbox. If it can't send it right away, it will stay here till it is sent.

The Ribbon

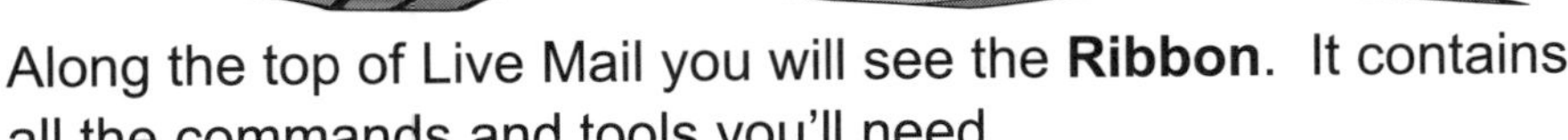

Along the top of Live Mail you will see the **Ribbon**. It contains all the commands and tools you'll need.

Everything is well organized under **Tabs**, in **Groups** of similar commands. Click on each tab and have a look!

Under the **Home tab**, you'll find all your everyday needs.

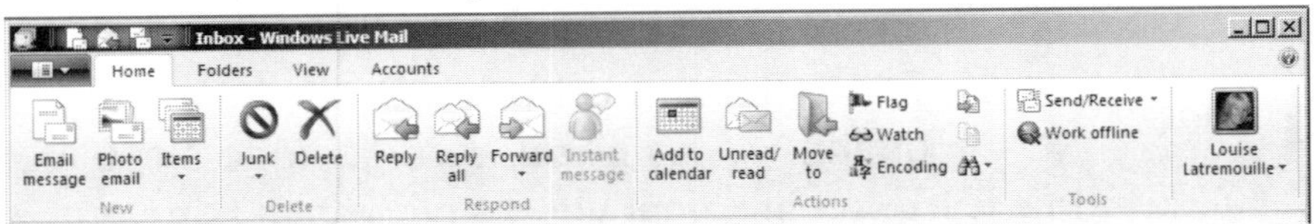

Under the **Folders tab** you'll find easy ways to find e-mails.

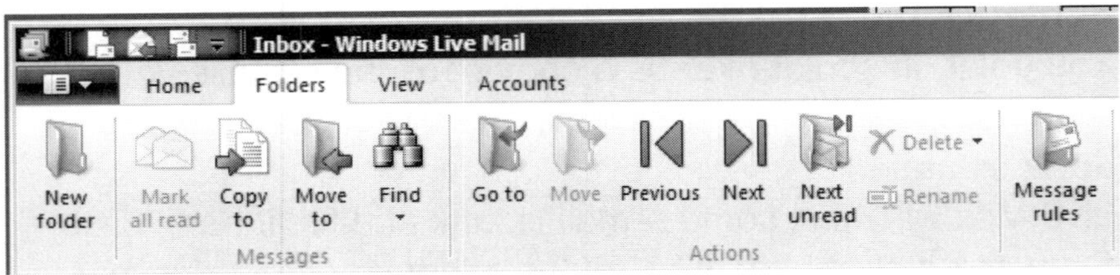

Under the **View tab** you can personalize how Live Mail looks.

The **Accounts tab** is where you go to add a new e-mail account. *Which is what we're going to do next!*

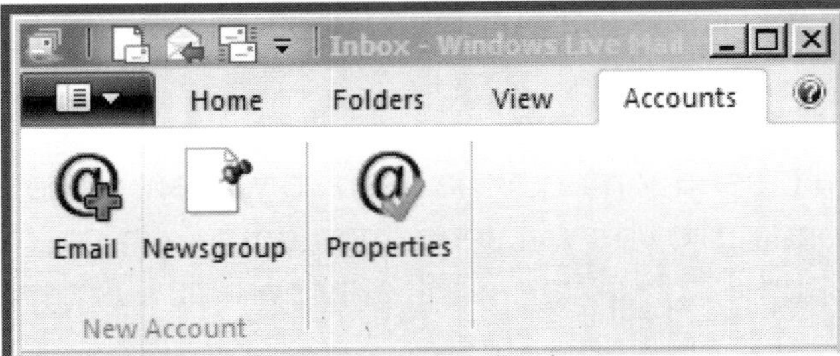

Click on the **Accounts tab** and you`ll see the tools to add an e-mail account, a newsgroup or see the properties of your existing e-mail accounts.

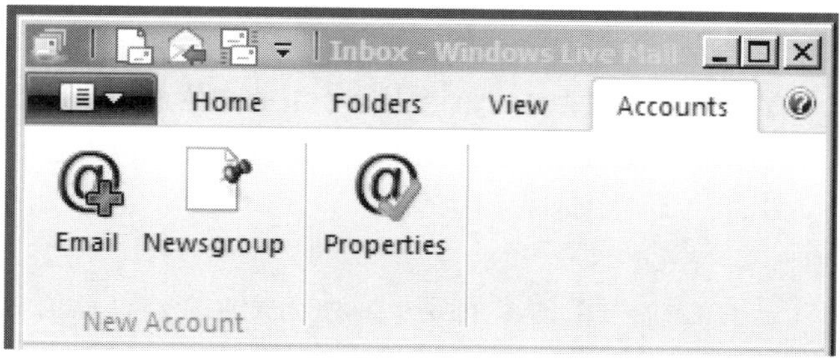

Click on Email. A wizard will open and you'll be walked through the steps to add an e-mail account. *When I say e-mail account, I also mean an e-mail address...*

♦ If the account you are adding is with your local server, you will need the settings we talked about earlier.
POP & SMTP

Generally, a local ISP will offer a number of free e-mail accounts. Nice, as you might want to set up individual addresses for different members of your family.

You can add e-mail accounts from other webmail servers as well, such as accounts from **Gmail, AOL and Yahoo!**
Here are the server addresses for those:

♦ **Yahoo!**: pop.mail.yahoo.com (incoming) and
smtp.mail.yahoo.com (outgoing)

♦ **AOL:** imap.aol.com (incoming) and
smtp.aol.com (outgoing)

♦ **Gmail:** pop.gmail.com (incoming) and
smtp.gmail.com (outgoing)

E-mail Accounts

If you have more than one e-mail account, under each one's name will be its own set of folders.

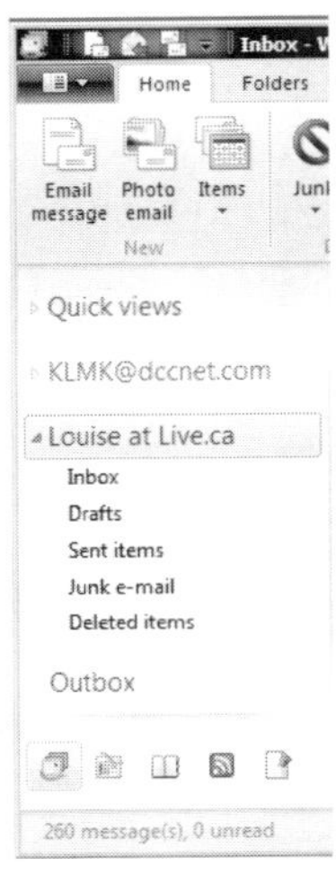

Here, I show two e-mail addresses. One with my local ISP and the other with Live Mail.

You can see or hide the folders for individual e-mail accounts by clicking on the little triangle that's beside its name.

E-mail sent to you at one address will go to the folders under its name.

Just above the e-mail account names you might see *Quick views.* In a few pages I show you how you can set up your options for Quick views.

If you created a Windows Live account, you will see it here, ready to go.

yourname@live.ca **or** yourname@hotmail.com

What a nice perk!

You don't need a Windows ID to use Live Mail.
You can use whatever e-mail address you want. *But...*

The Live Essentials programs work so well together.

They have a strong web component and use your Windows Live ID to tie things together. As we get further along, you'll see that if you want to use the programs to their fullest potential you are going to need a Windows Live ID.

You can get an ID anytime, by adding it through Accounts!

Just to recap what you do when you see instructions like this: Home > E-mail message

I want you to left-click through that path to get to the command we want.

When I write, Home > Email message, you should: Left-click on the *Home tab*, then on *Email message.*

Home Tab
The first *Group* under the Home tab is called *New.*

There are three common tools grouped with *New*.

Here's what's what:

Click on Email message to:
- ◆ Open a window to write a new e-mail.

Click on Photo email to:
- ◆ Write a new e-mail message that will include pictures from your computer.

Click on Items to:
- ◆ Add a new event to your Calendar,
- ◆ Add a new contact into your address book, or
- ◆ Send a new message to a Newsgroup that you are a member of.

Practice: New

Let`s write a new e-mail, then send and receive it.
After that, we`ll get more creative!

Click through this path to open a new e-mail window:
Home > Email message

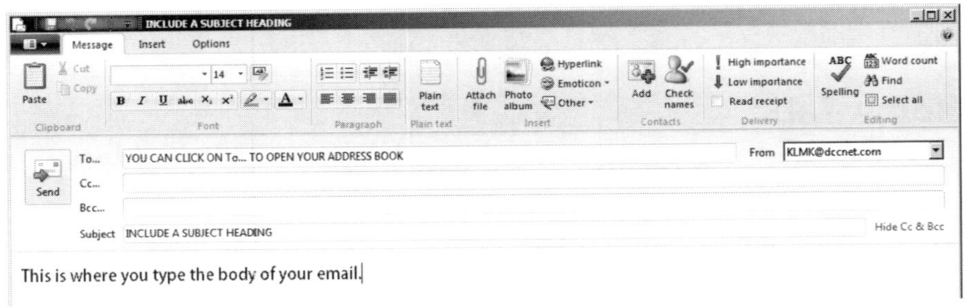

When your New message window first opens, your cursor will be blinking in the **To text box**, ready for you to type in a name or an e-mail address. Clicking on *To* will open Contacts, your address book, where you can search for a name or e-mail address that you've previously saved.

1. For our practice, type your e-mail address in the *To text box* . *Yes, you can e-mail yourself!*

2. Click your mouse into the text box beside *Subject* and type Practice.

3. Click your mouse into the main body of the e-mail and type, Well done!

4. To the left of *To*, you'll see the **_Send button_**. Click on the Send button. *Off it goes!*

Practice: Send/Receive

Live Mail can automatically check for new e-mail every 10 minutes or so, but you can check for e-mail manually as well.

Click through this path:
Home > Send & Receive

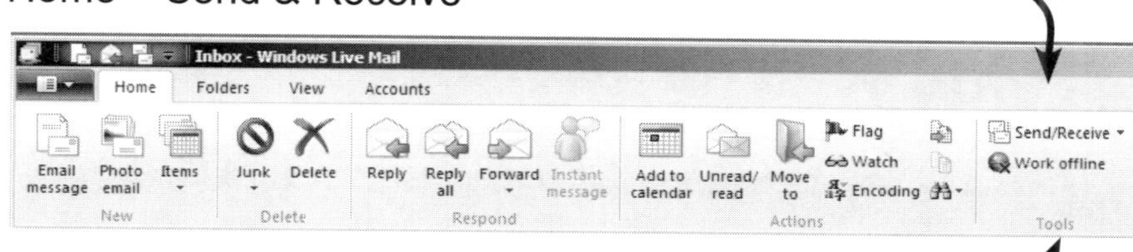

The Send/Receive tool is grouped with another tool, Work Off- or Online. This is the *Tools* group.

New mail has arrived!

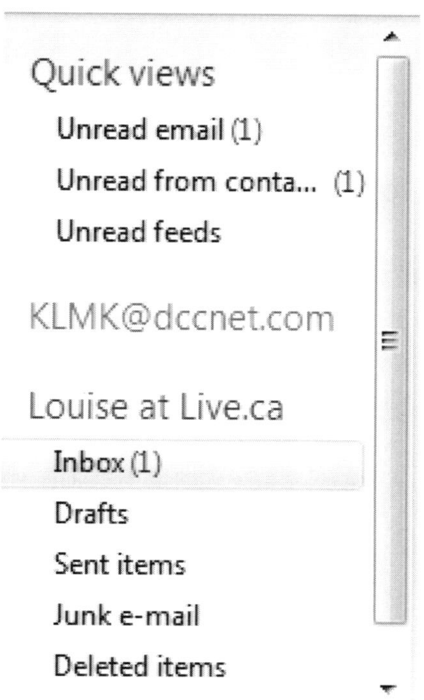

Quick views now shows (1) unread e-mail.

I have my own address in my address book, so I am a "contact". Therefore here, you also see (1) unread e-mail from contacts.

The Inbox, under the account I sent the e-mail to, shows (1).

You can click on Unread e-mail, Unread from contacts OR the Inbox to see the e-mail.

They all indicate you have received new unread mail.

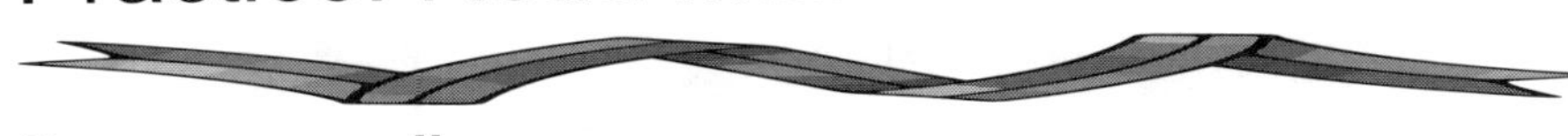

See your e-mail.

1. Click on your Inbox. It will become highlighted as soon as you click on it, letting you know that's the folder you're looking in.

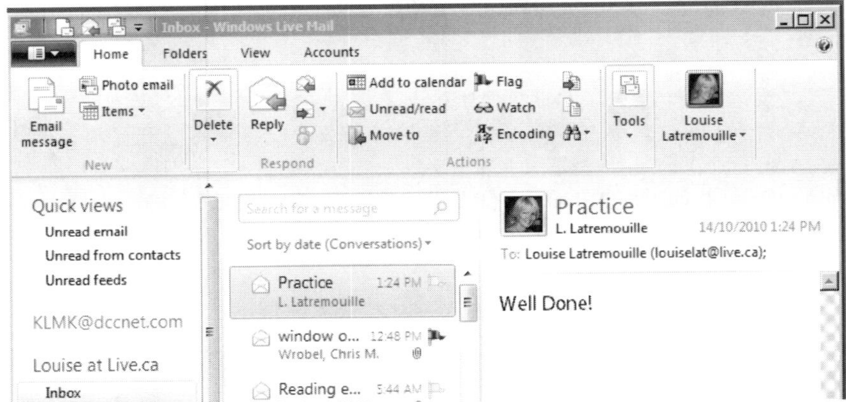

2. Click on "Practice" in the next column.
   - Notice that this column shows the subject of the e-mail and the sender's name. Once you click on an email, it becomes highlighted.
   - Unopened mail in your Inbox will show in **bold** print, after you view it, it turns to regular print.

3. Read your e-mail in the next column. Well done!

Now that you have read the e-mail, the 1's are gone beside the Inbox and Quick view folders. *No more unread e-mail...*

Want to write down a note or two?___________________

____

____

____

New Message Tools

These are the *Groups* at are on the top of the *New email message ribbon*. There are lots of tools to get creative!

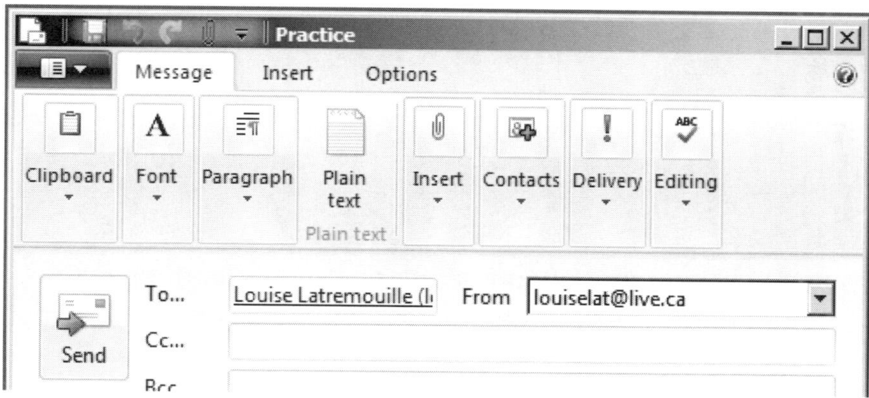

Here's what's what:

The Clipboard

If you *Cut* or *Copy* something, perhaps some text or a picture, it will be held on your Clipboard until you *Paste* it.

What's the difference between *Cut* and *Copy?*

When you *Cut* something, it is erased from where it was. When you *Copy* something, the original work stays put.

Here's how to Copy and Paste text:

1. Hold your left-click down and drag it over the text you want to copy. It will become highlighted.
2. Right-click to open a mouse menu and choose Copy.
3. Left-click your mouse where you want things copied to. Right-click again, choose Paste!

New Message Tools

Font

Font is typesetter lingo for what the text (typing) looks like.

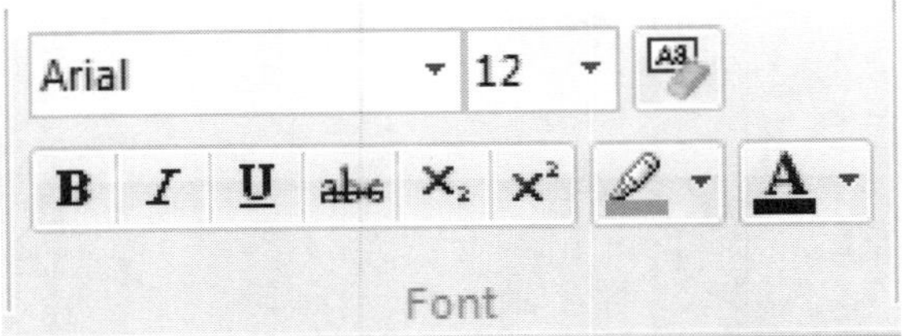

With these tools you can really format your e-mails to look funky!

You can click on an option first, then your typing after will have that effect. Or, you can highlight text and then choose an option; it will be applied to all the text that is highlighted.

Here's what's what:

♦ Click on the little arrow that's on the side of the box that says Arial and you will see a big list of fonts to choose from. This style of font is Arial.

♦ The 12 represents the size of font. This size is 12 pica. Click on the little arrow to adjust the size.

♦ The next little icon is an eraser. If you highlight text, then click on this, it will remove any fancy formatting.

♦ The **B** is for **Bold.**

♦ The *I* **is for making your text *Italic.***

♦ The U̲ is for underlining.

♦ The a̶b̶e̶ is for crossing out words.

♦ The X_2 will move your text a little below the line.

♦ The X^2 will move your text a little above the line.

♦ The next icon looks like a highlighter and that`s exactly what it does! You can even choose a color!

♦ Click on the **A** and you can choose from an array of colors for the font!

Paragraph

These tools are for **making lists and setting alignment**.

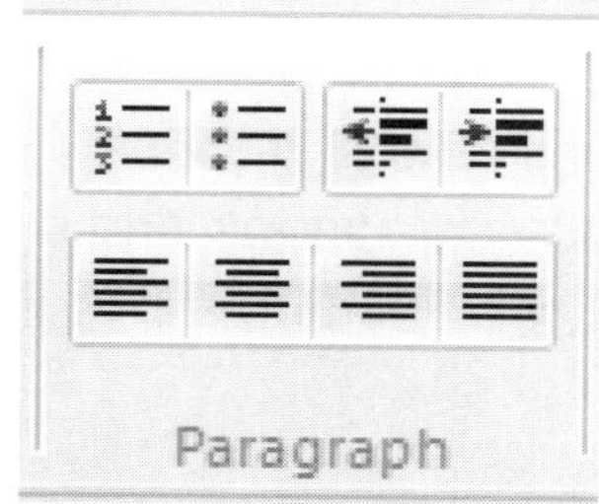

♦ Click on the 123 icon and you can make a numbered list.

♦ Click on the ... icon to make a bullet list. This is a type of bullet list.

♦ Click on the next two icons to move a block of text over to the right or to the left.

♦ The four icons on the bottom are all about how you want your paragraphs aligned. Either aligned on the left, centered, to the right, or justified in a block format.

This next Group will either say *Plain text or Rich text,* depending on which format you are typing in.

When you are typing in *Rich text* all the formatting options are available to use.

Click on *Plain text* to type e-mails without any special formatting. When you are typing in *Plain text*, this Group will say *Rich text* instead.

This is a sample **of** *Rich* *text*, **it has lots** of fancy formatting.

This is Plain text, it does not have any fancy formatting.

New Message Tools

Insert

This is where you find the tools to **attach files or photos** to an e-mail.

You will also find those fun little emoticons and the tool to include a link to a website.

♦ Click on *Attach file* and your Windows Explorer folder will open. From here you can browse for the file or files you want to attach.

♦ Click on *Photo album* to create a photo e-mail. I`ll talk lots more about Photo e-mails at the end of this chapter. For now you`ll just have to trust me, it`s a very cool tool!

♦ A *Hyperlink* is a link to a website. Click on this and you`ll open a small window where you'll type in the web address and if you want, a title or name for the link.

♦ *Emoticons* are smileys and such. 

♦ *Other* includes a tool to insert a horizontal line across your e-mail, and the tools to insert your e-business card or signature.

Wonder how to create a signature? It's an Option!

Go back to Mail's main screen.

Left of the Home Tab, you'll see a little icon with a wee arrow.

1. Click on the icon to open a menu.
2. In the menu, left-click on Options > Mail.
3. Click on the Signature tab in the window that opens and create away!

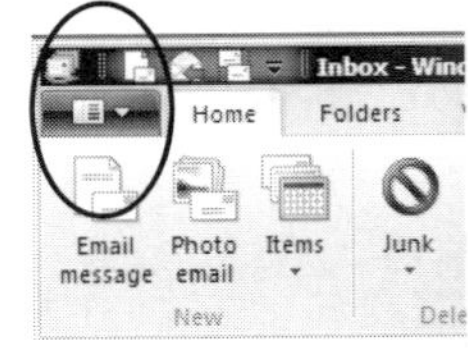

New Message Tools

The next group along the New message ribbon is **Contacts** *Contacts is your address book.*

There are three ways to open your Contacts folder:

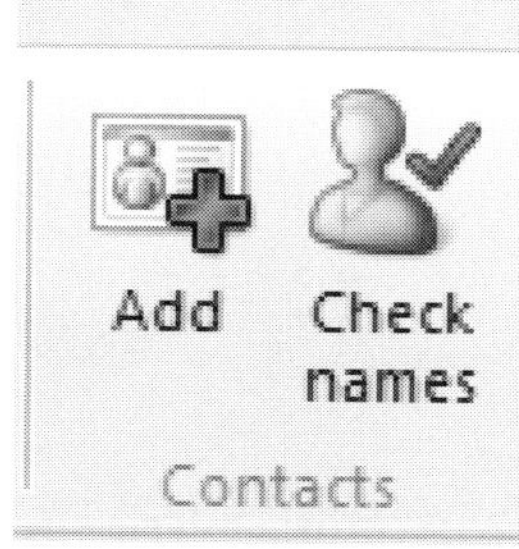

1. By clicking on *Add* along the ribbon.

2. By clicking on the *To, Cc or Bcc on a new e-mail.*

3. By clicking on the *Contacts icon that you can see* at the bottom of the first column .

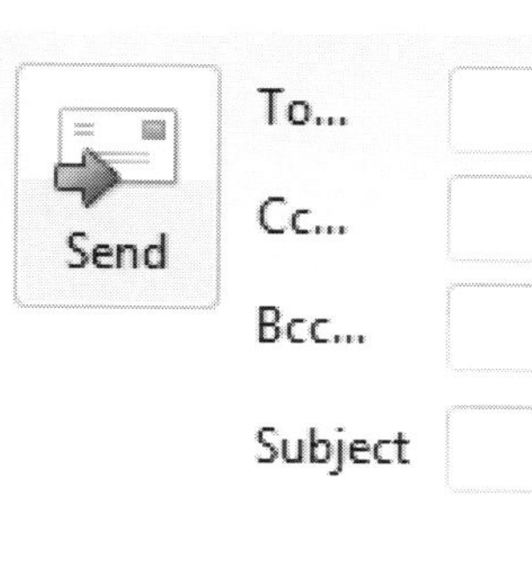

When you open your Contacts folder, you will see a list of all your saved entries (contacts).
To look for a contact, either:
♦ Type their name in the search window or,
♦ Grab the scroll bar that`s on the right side of the window and scroll up or down to see all your contacts.

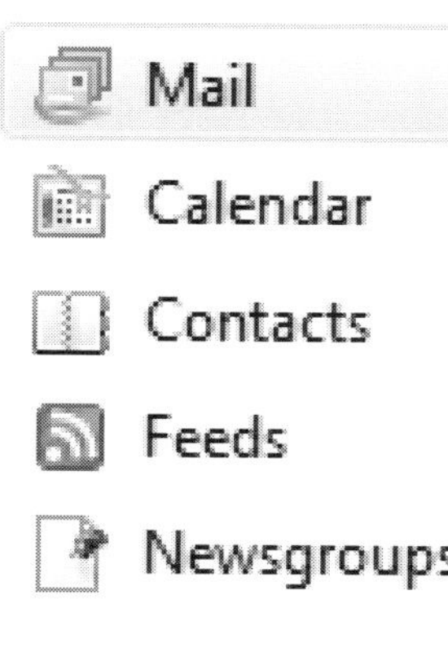

NOTE:
These icons open each part of the Live Mail program.

Click on Mail to use e-mail. Click on Calendar to use your Calendar, Contacts to open your address book, etc...

New Message Tools

The next group shows your **Delivery** tools.

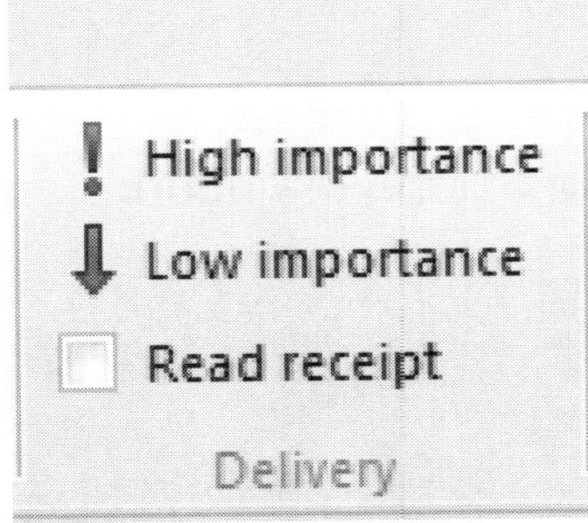

When you're ready to send an e-mail you can just send it. Or if you want, you can add one of these features.

Click on *High importance* and you will add some emphasis to the e-mail you are sending. (A very over-used tool) And I don't know why anyone would use *Low*... Here's an e-mail, don't care if you read it...?

If you click on *Read receipt*, when the receiver gets the e-mail they'll see an option where they can let you know if they got it. *They can choose* to send you the receipt, or ignore the request and read the e-mail anyway.

Got any Bright Ideas? ________________________

____

____

____

____

____

____

____

The *Editing* group.

The three tools on the right are pretty self explanatory...

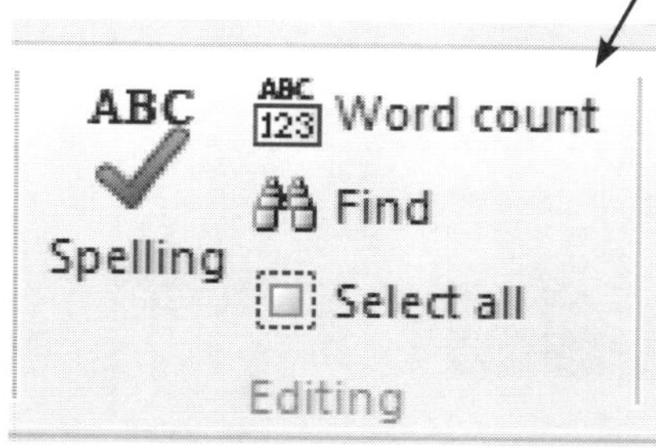

Word count, will count the words you've typed in your e-mail. ***Find*** will help you search for words in your e-mail and ***Select all*** will highlight your whole e-mail. Helpful to copy and paste!

> **Spelling is an Option.**
> **Remember how to set your Options?**
> To the left of the Home Tab, you'll see a little *Windows Live Mail icon* with a wee arrow.
> 1. Click on the *Windows Live Mail icon* to open a menu.
> 2. In the menu, click through:
>   Options > Mail > Spelling tab.

If you have *Spelling* enabled as one of your Options, Mail will check your e-mails for spelling before it sends them. *How nice!* Here's how it works:

As soon as Mail sees a spelling error it will draw a squiggly red line under the word, to draw your attention to it.

Spell check won't always be right though. For instance, my computer used to tell me Latremouille was a spelling mistake. Go figure! I had to *Add* my name to the dictionary so it would recognize it as correct. You might have to do the same!

New Message Tools

Click on *Spelling*, in the **Editing group**, to open this window.

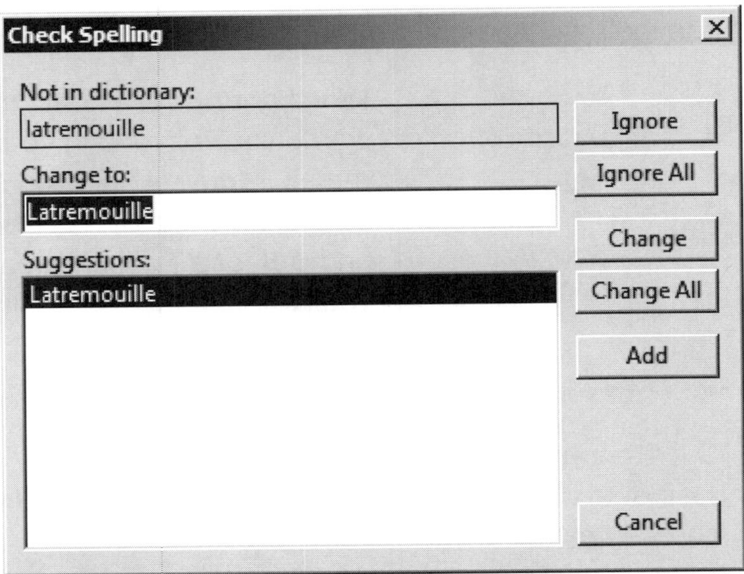

You'll see your misspelled word in the *Not in dictionary* box.

If Mail has any suggestions it'll show them in the bottom box. If you like the suggestion, highlight it and choose Change to automatically apply that choice.

The buttons on the right are plainly labeled. Click on:

♦ *Ignore*, if you DON'T want the word corrected.

♦ Ignore All, to ignore all of a particular mistake.

♦ *Change*, if you choose a suggestion and want it applied.

♦ *Change All,* if you want any recurring mistakes for that word corrected.

♦ *Add*, if you know the word is spelled correctly and you want to add it to the dictionary.

♦ *Cancel,* to close the window and not bother with Spelling.

Want to write down some notes?

Mail > Home Tab

We've just gone over the **New** group, found under the Home tab, and learned how to create and send an e-mail.
Now let's see what else is under the Home tab!

The **Home tab** holds the tools for your everyday needs.
On the next few pages we'll go over what's what.

To use a tool, you first have to select the e-mail you want to apply that command to.

How to select an email:

1. Click on the folder that the e-mail is in, maybe the Inbox.

    ♦   You will see the contents of that folder displayed in the next column. You can see the contents of the e-mail you select in the third column.

2. Click on an e-mail in the second column to select it.

    ♦   Now the tools up on the Ribbon are at your disposal!

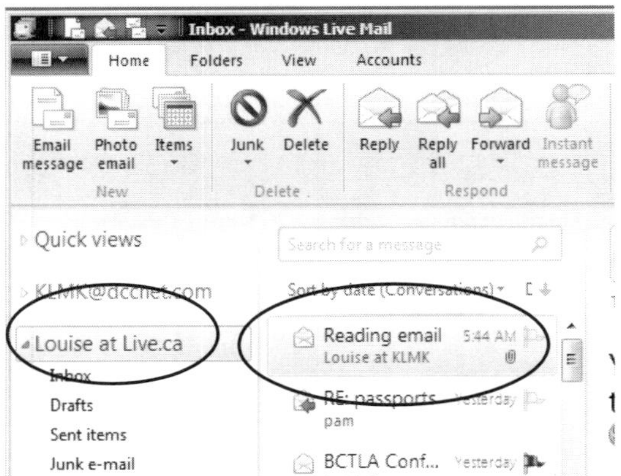

The next group under the home tab is **Delete**, where you'll find **Junk and Delete**.

Junk
Dunk your Junk!

♦ Select an e-mail.

♦ Click on the *Junk* icon.

♦ The e-mail will be moved into your Junk folder.

Control your Junk!
You can also choose what you would like to happen to any further e-mail that comes from a sender.

1. Select an e-mail.

2. Click on the little arrow below Junk to open your options.

3. Choose your poison!

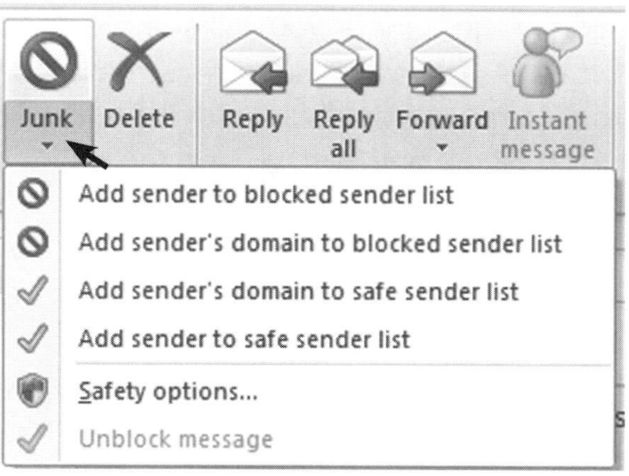

Some Junk's not Junk

One way that Mail helps keep you safe is by not downloading some e-mails entirely, until you say so. **Here's how and why:**

These are both the same e-mail.

See the banner at the top?

I clicked on Show and got the whole picture.

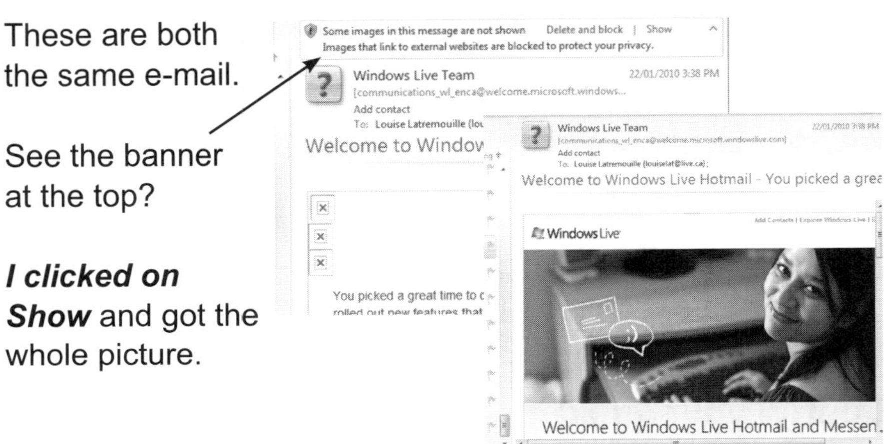

When downloading e-mail, Mail quickly scans for images that have links to websites embedded in them. If it finds any, you'll see a banner at the top of the e-mail that says:

"Some images in this message are not shown. Images that link to external websites are blocked to protect your privacy"

On the right side of the banner you will see the options:
Delete and block — This will delete the e-mail and then block any further e-mails from this sender. And,
Show — Click on Show and you will see the entire e-mail.

Just because Mail has blocked the images, doesn't mean the e-mail is bad or invasive; it only means that it has linked images.
For instance, I get my grocery store flyer e-mailed to me. Until I click on Show Images, I don't see the whole e-mail.
So, if you are interested in the information in the e-mail, click on Show and you'll get the whole story. *Simple as that.*

Delete

Click on an e-mail to select it, then click on Delete. Your e-mail is sent to the *Deleted items* folder. You can also delete an e-mail by selecting it, then press the delete key on your keyboard!

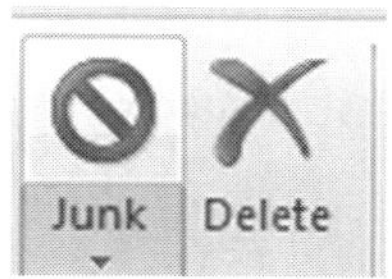

Delete something by mistake?

Don't worry, it's easy to get back. Here's how:

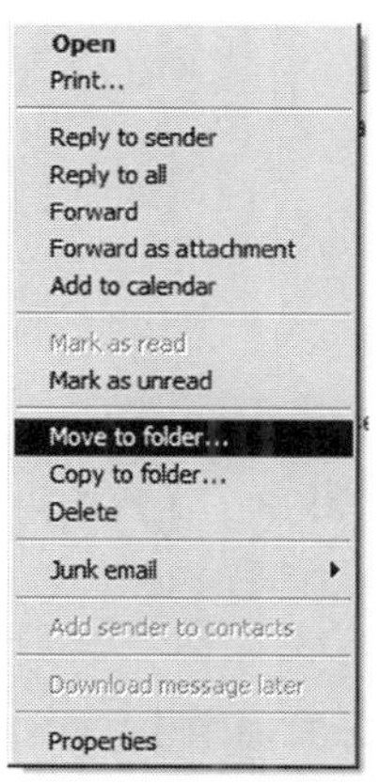

1. Click on the Deleted items folder to open it.

2. Right-click over the e-mail you want to retrieve.

3. Choose "Move to folder"

4. In the new window that pops up, highlight the folder you want it to go back to, then click OK.   *Zoom, back it goes!*

Keep your house clean - Keep your computer clean!
Remember to empty the trash!

Here's how to Empty your Deleted Items folder:

1. Right-click your mouse over "Deleted items" in the folders column to see what's in there.

2. Left-click your mouse over "Deleted items" and see the command "Empty the Deleted Items folder".

3. It will ask you "Are you sure you want to empty the Deleted Items folder?"... Click Yes.

When the Deleted items folder is emptied, things are gone, gone, gone. Never to be seen again.

Home > Respond

Respond is the next group along the ribbon.

You can *Reply, Reply All or Forward* any e-mail you receive. To use *Instant message*, both you and the sender must be members of Messenger.

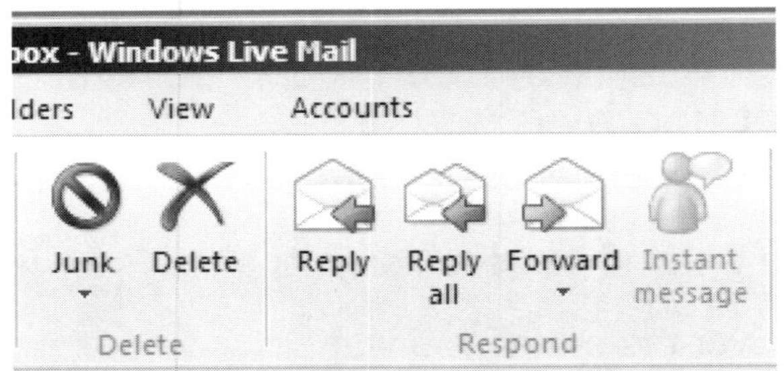

Reply

Click on Reply and a new e-mail will be created, already addressed to the sender!

Generally, e-mail that you reply to will contain a copy of the e-mail you are replying to. *But that's an Option!*

♦ Click on that little icon to the left of the Home tab to open Mail's menu, then: Options > Mail > Send. Tick or un-tick "Include message in reply".

Personally, I like it when the original mail is included in replies...

Reply All

Reply All is a great tool if you are working with a group. If you have received an e-mail that was sent to a group of people, click on "Reply all" and your reply will be sent to everyone.

Forward

If you've received an e-mail that you want to forward on to someone else, this is the tool for you! When you receive a forwarded e-mail, you will see fwd in the subject line.

>When you create or receive forwarded e-mail, often bullets
>will show up at the beginning of each line; like what I show
>here.
>
>**Tip**
>**If you want to get rid of these bullets, >> use**
>**Copy/Paste. Here's how:**

1. Hold down the left-click on your mouse and drag it across the part of the of the e-mail you want to copy, to highlight it.

2. Once highlighted, right-click and choose Copy.

3. Create a new e-mail

4. Click your mouse into the body of the new e-mail and right-click again, to open the mouse menu.

5. Left-click on Paste.

Home > Actions

Actions is the next group along the ribbon.
Here's what's what:

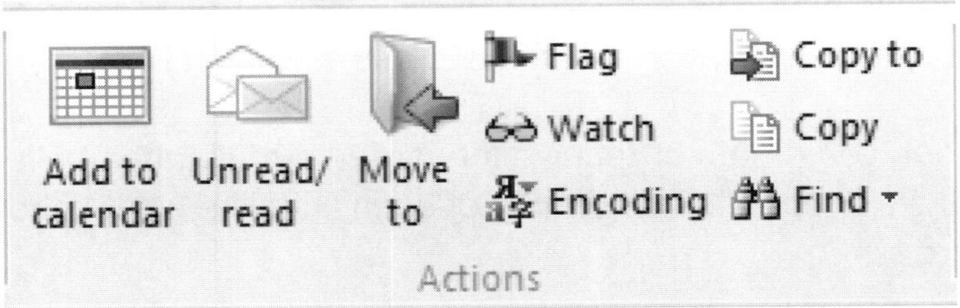

Add to calendar	Click on this and you can add the e-mail as an event on your calendar. More on how the Calendar works coming up.
Unread/read	Click on this and you'll change the status of an e-mail from Unread (shown in bold) to read — or vice versa.
Move to	Click on this to move an e-mail from one folder to another.
Flag	Click on this to make the flag beside its Subject turn red.
Watch	Click on this and the Subject of the e-mail will turn red.
Encoding	This has to do with *character set* (letters and numbers in an alphabet). English encoding is usually Western European.
Copy to	Click on this to copy an e-mail to another folder.
Copy	Click on this and you will copy an entire e-mail, ready to paste it into another e-mail or document.
Find	Great for finding words in an e-mail or helping you find a certain e-mail message.

Tools is the next group along the ribbon. It's where you'll find *Send/Receive* and the option to *Work offline*.

You can instantly send or check for mail by clicking on the *Send/Receive* tool.

By default, Mail will automatically check for new e-mail every 5 or 10 minutes. But, you can change this setting. **Checking for Mail is an Option, under the General tab.**

Set your Options!

To the left of the Home Tab, you'll see a little *Windows Live Mail icon* and a wee arrow.
1. Click on the *Windows Live Mail icon* to open a menu.
2. In the menu, click through:

> Options > Mail > General tab

While you're here...

You may have noticed that I've mentioned setting your options a couple of times already... Have a look around at the other options. Click on the tabs and see what's under them.

I can't tell you how many times I've been frustrated at my computer because it's doing something for no apparent reason. Then I discovered Options!

Life's not so frustrating any more.

Home > Account

The last group is all about you!

This shows if you are signed into a *Live Account* or not.

Click on the little arrow to View and/or edit your Profile or Live Account info.

You can sign-out of Live Mail here, as well as sign-in with a different Windows Live ID.

Want to write down some bright ideas? _______________

____

____

____

____

____

____

____

____

____

____

The **Folders tab.**

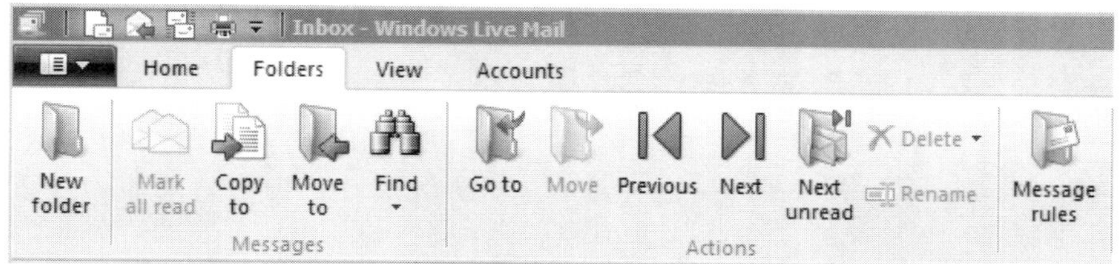

What's what:

♦ The tools in the **Messages** and **Actions** groups are so straight-forward they don't really need explaining. They do exactly what they say.

♦ As for **New folder** (on the left side) and **Message rules** (on the right side), they can work together... Here's an example:

   ♦ Perhaps you're organizing a high school reunion. You might receive many e-mails from people you don't generally associate with and you don't want to lose any of these e-mails in your regular inbox folder. You can create a special folder just for these e-mails!

   ♦ With Message rules, you can create a rule that when an e-mail comes in with the subject "Reunion", it would go directly to that folder.

   This is just an example; there are infinite scenarios that you might find yourself wanting help organizing your e-mails with. If you do, have a look around under the Folders tab!

View Tab

Under the **View tab** you'll find tools to personalize Mail. Try the different views out, it's easy to change things back.

New view.
What *New view* does is hide e-mail that has been read. Or maybe a better way to explain it, is to say that when you click on *New view,* you'll only see new, unread mail.

View
Find the tools here to set conditions for flagging messages.

Quick views
This is handy. I have my Quick view folder to show only new unread mail, but you can set it to show all sorts of things. Click on this tool to see your options!

Filter messages
This is kinda like *New view.* You can choose to view or hide messages.

View > Arrangement

The next group, **Arrangement**, has some handy tools!

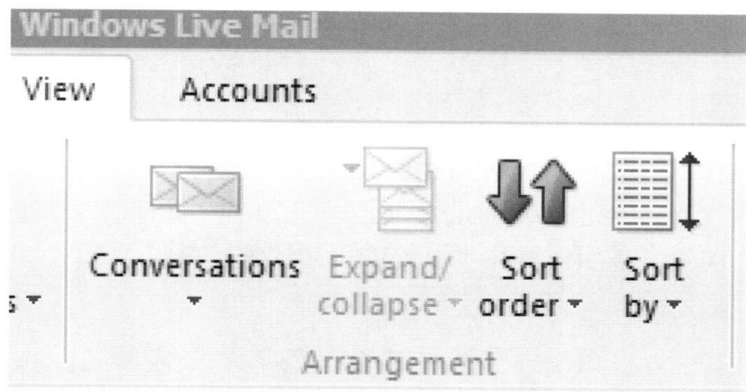

Conversations

When *Conversations* is turned on, e-mails that are in reply to one another are threaded and grouped together in your message list.

When *Conversations* is turned off, reply e-mails are not threaded together.

Expand/collapse

If you have Conversations turned on, you can use this to hide or show all the previous e-mails in a conversation group.

This all makes so much more sense when you try it. So go ahead! Try it out.

Sort order

You can choose by Ascending or Descending order, depending on how you choose to *Sort by...*

Sort by

You can sort your e-mails by date, who they are from, the subject... lots of options here. Pick and choose! It's a good tool to help find lost e-mails.

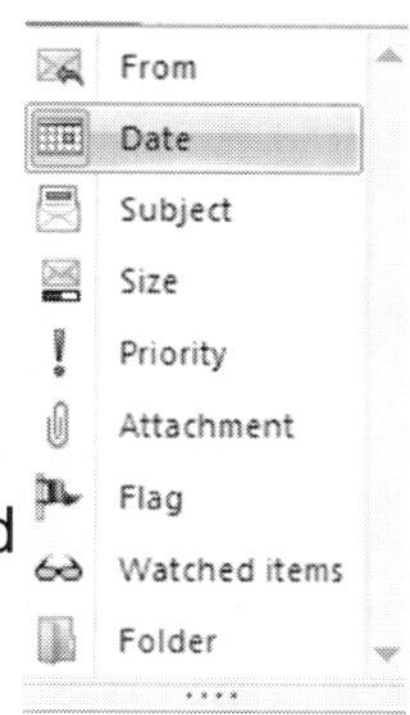

View > Layout

The ***Layout group*** is for how you want Mail to look.

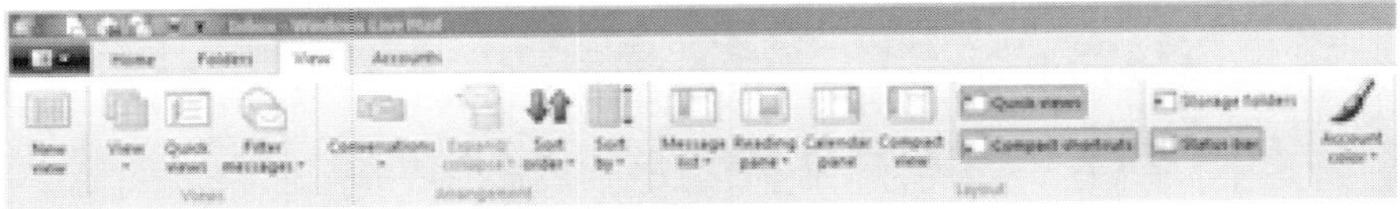

You can change the Mail's layout anytime, as often as you like. To change how Mail is laid out, just click on one of the layout options and see how Mail looks. *Try them all out!*

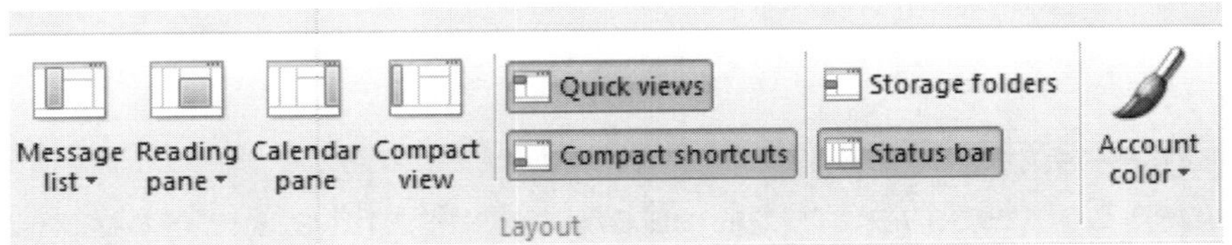

Message list
View your messages listed on one or two lines. Easier to see than explain, try it out and you'll see what I mean.

Reading pane
Read highlighted messages in a column to the right side of the message list or in a pane below the list. Or, choose not to see the messages at all, by turning the option off.

Calendar pane
You can choose to view you Calendar on the right side or not. You can even compact the folders on the left side if you want.

Quick views, Compact shortcuts, Storage folders & Status bar
Click on these buttons to show or hide the features. For instance, click on Quick views and you'll either *show* or *hide* Quick views in the left sidebar.

Account Color
You can change the color of your e-mail accounts!

Bright Ideas

Want to write down some notes?

Attaching Pictures and Files

I mentioned earlier that we'd get into attaching files and pictures to an e-mail. Here we are, already!

On the next few pages I'll show you:
- ◆ Why sometimes size matters.
- ◆ The difference between attaching a file and creating a photo e-mail.
- ◆ How to browse for files and pictures.
- ◆ How to fancy up a photo e-mail.
- ◆ How to open attachments.

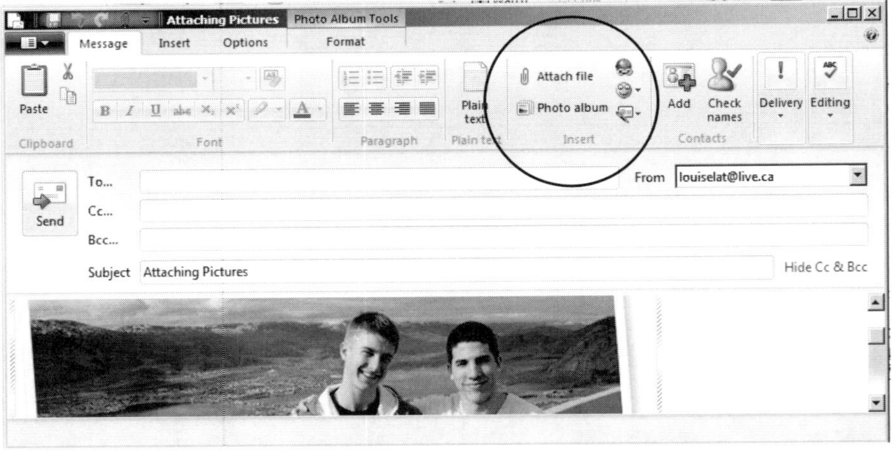

When you send an e-mail with attachments, you should think of the computer that is receiving it too.

Be nice to your friends...
If the file you are attaching is large, don't send it to someone who has a slow internet connection. It could really bung up their system.

Before we get going...
A little of *"Things you don't really need to know, but knowing will help everything make more sense"* ...

Sending and Receiving Photos

How fast an e-mail can be sent or received, depends on a few things:

1. How fast the computers sending AND receiving are.

2. How fast the internet connections are. Dial-up is very slow, Cable and DSL connections are fast.

3. How large the e-mail is. (How much *data* the e-mail contains.)

♦ Photos can be large files. Large files can take a long time to send or to receive. *Be a friend. If someone has a slow internet connection, don't e-mail them large files. It'll totally bung up their system.*

♦ In computer terms, the size of a file depends on how much data it has.

♦ A high definition photo has lots of data, so it's a large file.

♦ A low resolution photo has less data, so it's a smaller file.

♦ In terms of size and data... 1 MB (Megabyte) equals about 1,000 KB (Kilobytes).

♦ The average size of a regular picture from a digital camera is around 2 to 4 **MB**s.

♦ The average size of a one page Word document is 40 **KB**s.

About Photo E-mails

When you send a photo as an attachment, an exact copy of the file is attached. If the photo is 3MB, 3MB is attached.

When you create a "photo e-mail", you send small, thumbnail versions of your pictures.

So, instead of attaching a 3 MB picture which might take 2 or 3 minutes to download, the thumbnail might only be 300 KB; *a tenth of the size and only take a few seconds to download!*

If you are signed into your Windows Live account, when you send a photo e-mail only thumbnails get e-mailed. ***But,* full-size, high definition versions of your pictures are stored on the Windows Live server for a month.**

This allows the receiver to go online and view or download the *high-def* versions of the pictures you sent!

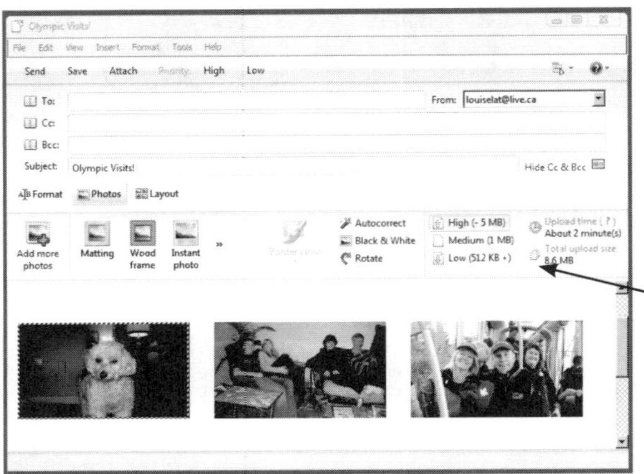

You can adjust the size of the picture files you are sending!

E-mail High Medium or Low resolution pictures.

You can attach pictures to your e-mails two ways.

♦ You can turn the message into a photo e-mail.

♦ Or, you can attach an image file to an e-mail.

"Attaching a file" is the more traditional way, so we'll go over that first. **Here's how to attach a file to an e-mail:**

1. Open an e-mail to send. It can be a New e-mail or you might want to Reply to someone. ☺

2. Click on *Attach file* to open Windows Explorer and browse for the file.

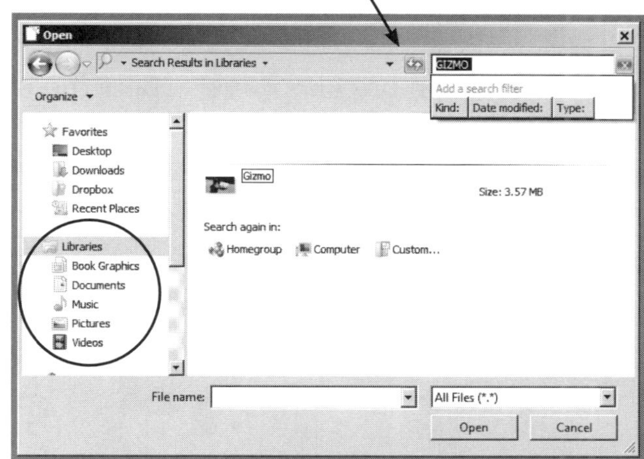

3. *If you know the file's name,* the easiest way to find it is to type its name the Search window.

3. *If you don't know the file's name,* browse thumbnails!

Use the view option of "*icons*" and you will see little thumbnails of your pictures. Click here to change your view.

Seeing thumbnails is a great way to search for pictures.

You'll have to choose what folder to look in.

Browse for Pictures

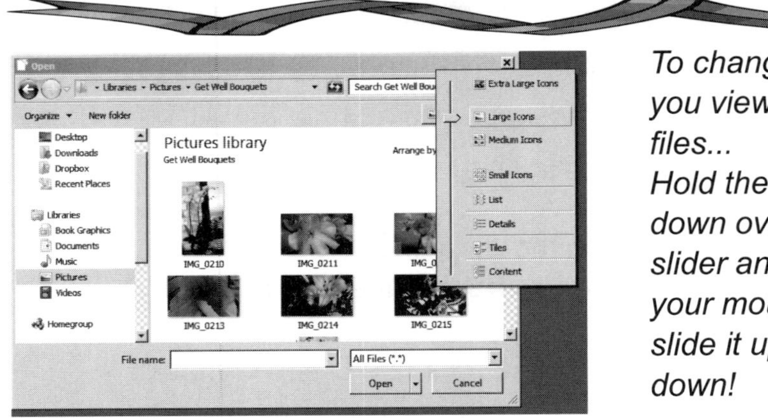

To change how you view your files...
Hold the left-click down over the slider and move your mouse to slide it up and down!

4. When you see the picture or file you want, click on it.

♦ Double-clicking on the file will attach it to your e-mail, or once it's selected, you can click on "Open" to attach it.

Zoom, back you go to your e-mail.

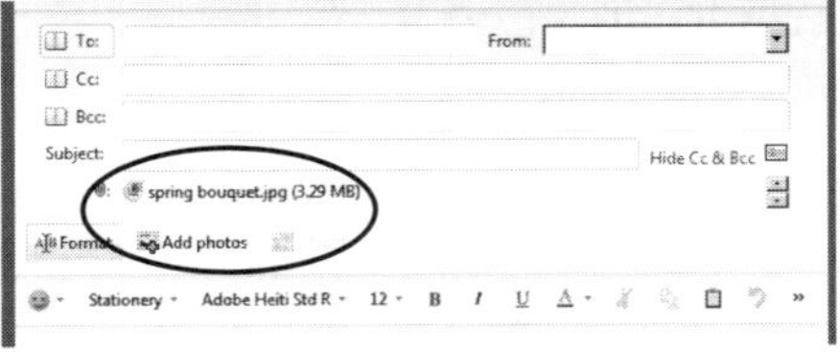

See the file you attached? *It's right below the Subject line.*

Want to attach more files? Just repeat the steps...

Next — Creating a photo e-mail!

Practice Photo E-mail

Let's Practice!

Here's how:

1. Open a new e-mail and address it to yourself, then type *Photo e-mail* in the Subject line.

2. *Click on Photo album.* Your Pictures folder should open up, but if it doesn't, browse to the folder your pictures are in.

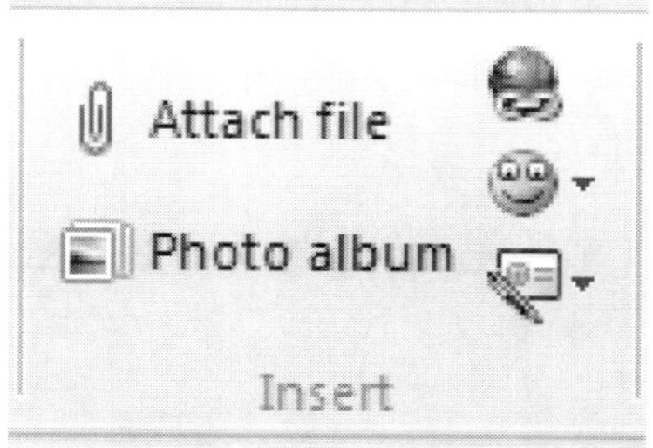

3. Double click on a picture to insert it in your e-mail.

4. Back in your e-mail you'll see the picture and a few options. Click on Enter album name to rename it.

Enter album name here

Want to add more photos? Click here.

Have a look at the top of your e-mail. Notice that the tabs have changed to reflect what you need for a Photo e-mail.

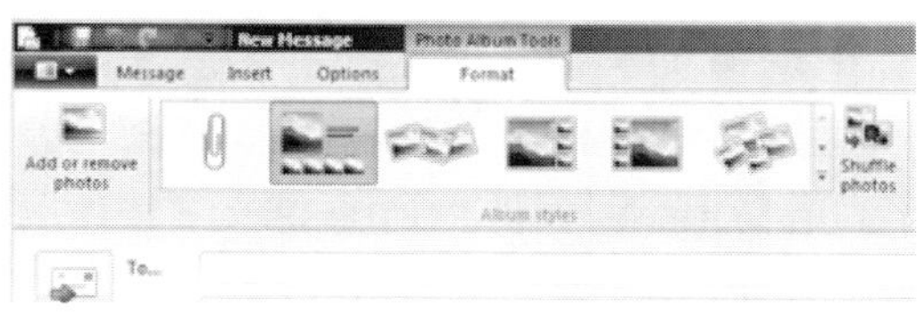

Practice Photo Album

After you choose your pictures, click around on the options you have here. It's fun to see all the different layouts.

See the paperclip? You can attach a file to a photo e-mail too.

You can add more, or remove pictures. You can even change the order they are in by clicking on Shuffle photos.

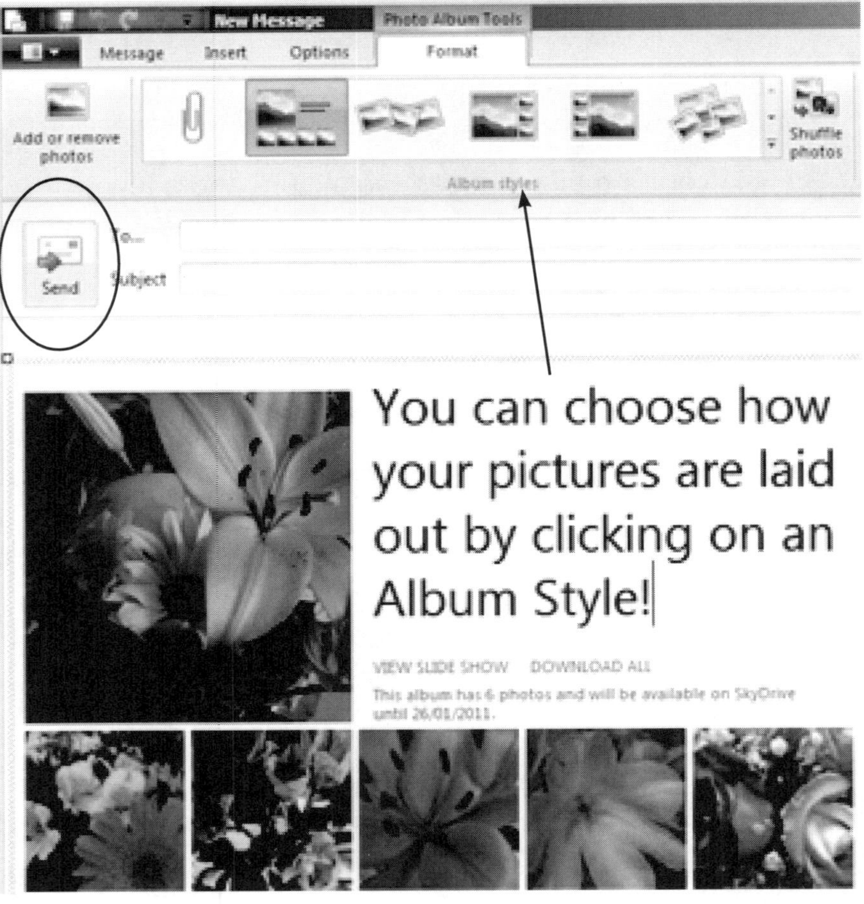

5. Is your e-mail addressed? If not, address it to yourself and then, click on Send!

Let's Practice, continued...

6. Click Home > Send/receive to check for new e-mail. Click on the e-mail to open it.

You can view all the pictures in the e-mail as is, or you can view the full-size pictures online.

♦ Click on VIEW SLIDE SHOW and you will automatically go on-line, to the Live Gallery website SkyDrive, to view the high-def versions of the pictures. From here you can pick and choose which of the pictures you want to download. Hover your mouse over the top part of the pictures to see a toolbar that hides & shows.

♦ If you want to Download high-def versions of all the pictures, click on DOWNLOAD ALL.

♦ Pictures in photo e-mail are *linked* to the Live server where their full size versions will be stored for a month or two.

♦ The recipient does not need a "Live" account to view or save the high-def versions of the pictures you send them in a Photo e-mail.

...Ding Dang Dong, that's cool!

Attachments

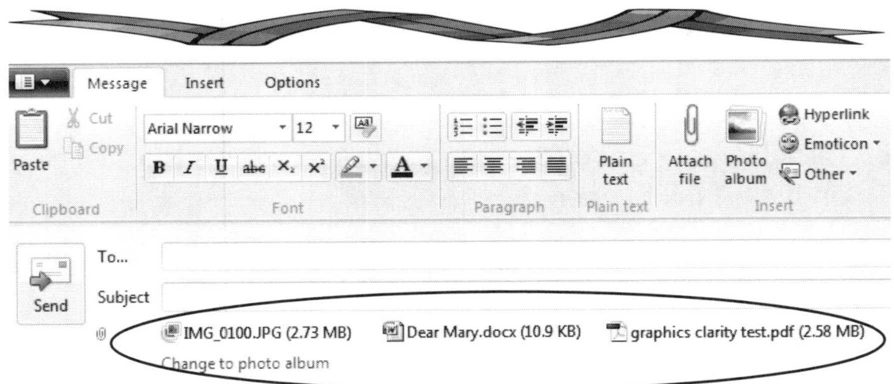

These files are all attached to an e-mail. They are all different types of files. A .jpg is an image file, .docx is a Word document file and .pdf is an Adobe pdf file.

Here's how to open an attachment:
Different types of files are opened by different types of programs. If you don't have a compatible program for the type of file you've been sent, you might not be able to view it.

Double-click over an attachment to open it. Your computer will look to see if it has the right program to open it with.

Here's how to save an attachment:

1. Right-click over the attachment.

2. In the menu that opens, left-click over Save as...

3. Your *Windows Explorer* window will open. Click on the Library you want to save the file in.

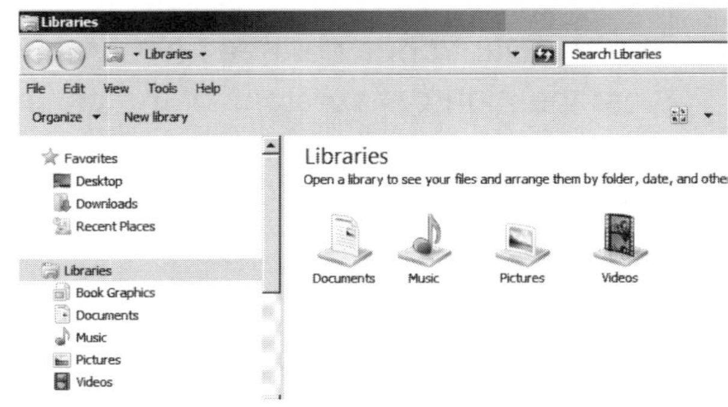

4. You can rename the file or leave it as is.

5. Click on Save.

Feeds and Newsgroups

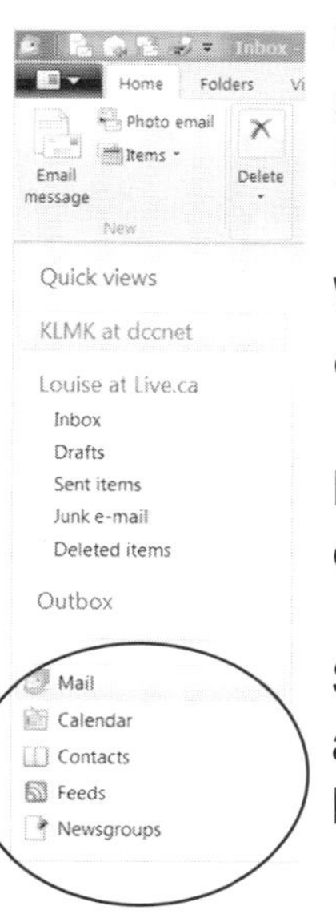

On the bottom of the left sidebar you will see Mail, Calendar, Contacts, Feeds and Newsgroups.

When you are using e-mail, Mail must be clicked on to open the e-mail windows.

If you want to use the calendar you have to click on Calendar to open it.

Same goes with opening Contacts (your address book) or looking at your Feeds or Newsgroups.

You'll either see the *expanded view* like above, or just the icons like this.

To change from one view to the other, hold your mouse just above where Mail is... *Wait a sec*... Then click, when you see the little green arrow appear.

Are you a news junkie?

You might like Feeds.

Feeds and Newsgroups

Feeds

Feeds are like news headlines or updates from websites. News and magazine websites often have feeds that you can subscribe to.

Somewhere on your internet browser you'll see this icon. It's along the right side of the toolbar if you're using Internet Explorer. It's up in the address bar if your using Firefox.

When you are on a website that has a feed to offer, the icon turns a color, otherwise it just looks greyed out.

To subscribe to a feed, just click on the icon. You'll go to a subscription page and click on "subscribe". It's that easy.

New feeds will be directed to Feeds in Mail where you can view them at your leisure. *Feeds are usually, always, free!*

Newsgroups

Newsgroups, as a name, is a little misleading. They are more like message boards. And finding what you're looking for can be a little like looking at an overcrowded bulletin board at your local supermarket.

But... Say you're part of a club. Someone might want to start a Newsgroup so your club members can post or answer questions etc. For this, Newsgroups are a nice!

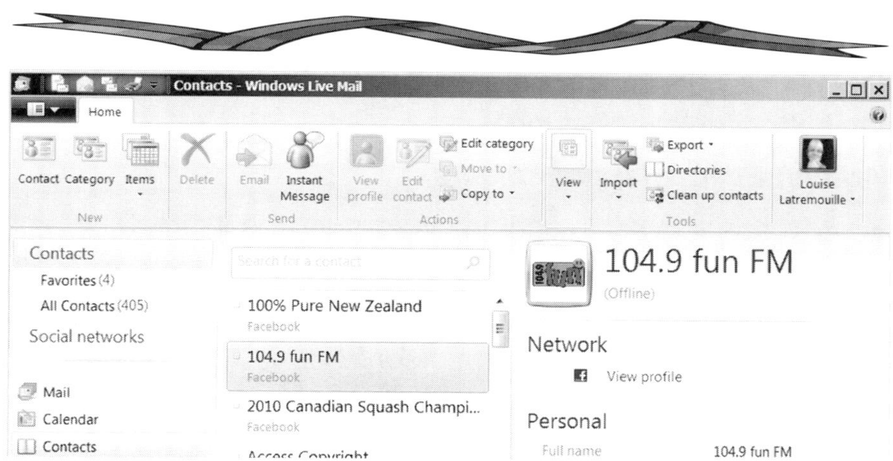

Contacts is your address book! Here are some pointers:

♦ Click on the *Contacts icon* at the bottom of the left sidebar to open your address book.

♦ When *Contacts* is open you will see your contacts listed in the center column. Click on a contact's name to see their details in the right column.

♦ *To add a new contact*, click on *Contact* in the **New group**, (on the left side of the ribbon).

♦ *To create a distribution list* click on *Category,* in the **New group.** You might want to create a category for a club e-mail list or perhaps one that includes just your family members. Creating a Category (distribution list) saves you typing out a bunch of addresses separately on an e-mail.

♦ You can Import e-mail addresses from other sources. Click on Import and you'll be walked through the steps.

♦ Use Export to create a backup of your address book. *A .CSV file can be read by Excel or Word.*

♦ Your *Contacts* are associated with the *Live ID Account* you are signed in to when you add them. If you tend to sign in to different accounts, you might end up having your contacts spread around in *different Live ID Accounts...*

The Calendar

Open Calendar by clicking on Calendar's icon, found in the bottom of the left sidebar.

Adding Events (appointments)

- The easiest way to add an event is to type it directly in a date square.

- The easiest way to include the time for an event is to click on the date with Calendar in *Month view*, then change to *Day view* to see all the times!

- You can move events around by grabbing them with your mouse!

- If you want to be e-mailed a reminder about an event, double click on the event to open the *Events window.* Notice at all your options here on the Events tab ribbon.

- Is it a recurring event? Click on *Recurring* on the ribbon in the *Events window* to see what you can do! I've got "water plants" recurring weekly on my calendar...

- Click on *Calendar,* under the Home tab, to color-code events.

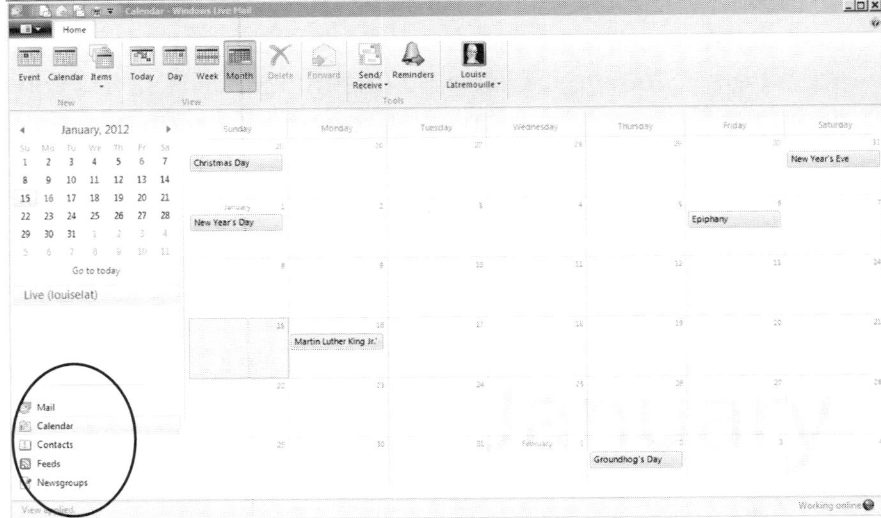

The Calendar

The On-line Calendar is super!

When you are signed into your Live Account, Calendar has some super on-line capabilities.

1. Go to *www.live.com* and sign-in to your Live or Hotmail account.

2. Once there, look for "Calendar". It will be either on the left sidebar or click on Hotmail > Calendar.

♦ Calendar, in your computer, syncs immediately with your Live account. The on-line calendar and the calendar on your computer will always reflect one another.

♦ Through the Live servers, you can access your calendar from any on-line device. *Handy if you are not at home!!*

♦ You can "share" your calendar with other people that have Live accounts. *Nice for coordinating busy families!*

♦ You can "Subscribe" or "download" specialty calendars. Calendars you download must be in an *.ics* format, because that's what Calendar uses! Look for and click on Subscribe on the toolbar and see what calendars show up as available in your area.

When You're Away from Home

You can check your Live Mail account anywhere you can access the internet.
Go to:

http://login.live.com

On the page that opens, you will see a couple sign-in options.

If you are NOT using your own computer, for extra security, click on this option: "Get a single use code to sign in with".

If you are using your own computer, sign in with your Windows Live ID, *which is your Live or Hotmail e-mail address*, and your password.

On the page that opens, click on Hotmail to check your mail.

Checking local ISP e-mail when you're away from home...
If you have e-mail accounts with your local ISP, you have to log onto *their webmail service* to access any new e-mail sent to you at that address. **Here's why:**

Live Mail is web-based e-mail.
When you sign-in to you@live.ca or you@hotmail, you log directly onto the Windows Live server, where your web-based e-mail folders are always accessible, along with your Contacts, Calendar, Feeds and Newsgroups.

Local e-mail servers are usually home-based.
E-mail sent to this address — you@yourISP.com — generally, are only on your ISP's server only until they are download into your home computer.

How to check for home-based e-mail when you're away, next!

Local Webmail Service

Most local ISP`s offer some sort of webmail service so you can check incoming mail when you are away from home.

you@yourISP.com

Here's how to log-on to a local webmail service:

1. Go on-line and search for:
   www.webmail.*NameOfYourServer*.com

   When you see your server's webmail site, click on it to open the page.

2. On the page that opens, you'll enter your username and password to open your server's webmail page.

Username		(Your e-mail address)
Password		

The password is the one you set up with your local server.

That's it!
Its not like using your own e-mail program, but your can send and receive new e-mails here. You'll have to look around to familiarize yourself with how the page is set up... where the Send button is, etc. But I bet you will find it pretty easy to use.

Unlike the Live mail server, you might only see newly received e-mail here. Local servers only have so much space dedicated to your personal Inbox. So when e-mail is downloaded to a computer at home, it's often erased from their server. Freeing up the space again.

Bright Ideas

Want to write down some notes?

Windows Live Photo Gallery

Feel like a pro!

Windows Live Photo Gallery

Windows Live Photo Gallery

Photo Gallery is not a big complicated photo editing program. It does good, basic photo editing and a terrific job organizing your photos. It's easy to download photos into, and easy to e-mail photos with.

Did you install Windows Live Photo Gallery when you installed Live Mail? If you didn't, install it now! Installing directions back on page 47...

How to open Windows Live Photo Gallery

1. Click on the Start menu and type "Photo" in the search window. Photo Gallery will show up somewhere in the menu above it.

2. Move your mouse over *Windows Live Photo Gallery* and click to open.

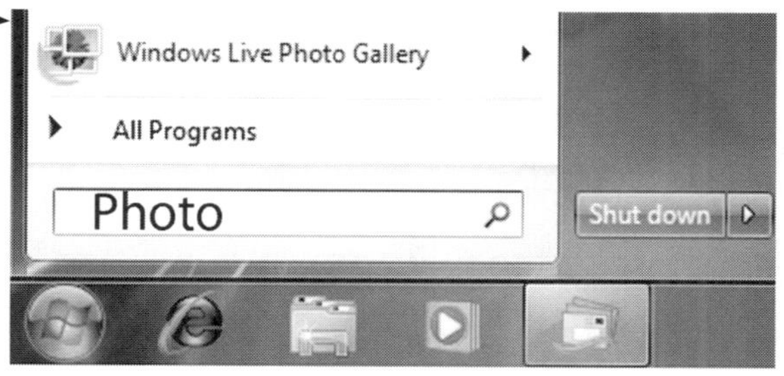

It might be nice to create a shortcut to his program. Remember how? Directions back on page 50.

- ◆ Right-click on Windows Live Photo Gallery
- ◆ Choose either:
        "Pin to Start Menu" *or* "Pin to Taskbar"

Setup

Want to make life easier in the future?
Personalize Photo Gallery! Here's how:
Same as with Live Mail, click on the little icon left of the Home
tab to open the Photo Gallery's menu, then click *Options.*

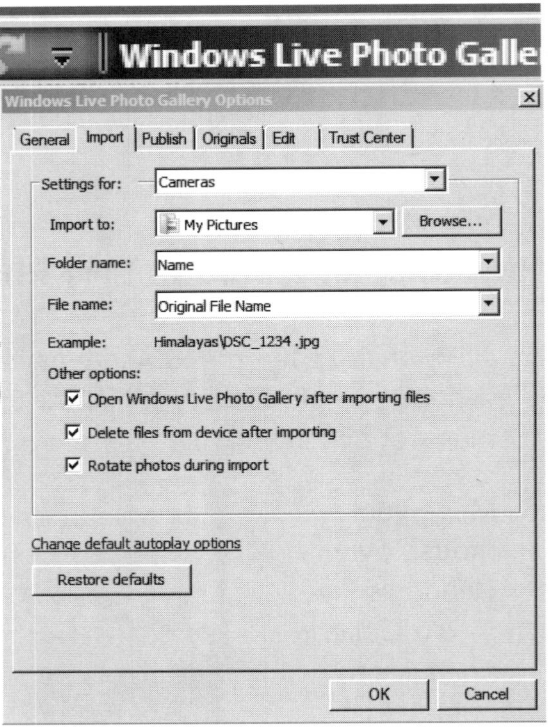

- Click on each of the Option tabs.

- Read what's under each tab.

- Choose the Options you want!

- You'll discover that this is where you set up where pictures will be saved in your computer.

- As well as whether or not to automatically rotate pictures when you import them.

Now...
Let's import some pictures
from your camera!

How to import pictures from your camera.

1. Open Photo Gallery.

2. Connect your camera to your computer. This is usually done with a USB cord that came with your camera. One end will be specific to your camera, the other a USB.

3. Turn your camera on and set it to View mode — as if you were scrolling through the pictures on your camera.

4. If the import does not start automatically, click on Import, under the Home tab.

5. A window will open that should show your camera. Make sure the camera is highlighted, then click Import.

6. In the next window you can name the album if you like or, Photo Gallery will name the folder/album it creates for the new pictures with the date.

7. **Click on More Options**, at the bottom of this window to see what's available, you might like what you see!

8. Click on Import.

♦ First the pictures all get imported. **_Then,_** if you chose to delete the pictures from your camera, it does that next.

> Deleting the pictures from your camera
> after the pictures are imported
> erases the memory card in your camera,
> making it ready to start fresh all over again. ♥

Memory Cards

A camera is not the only thing you can download pictures from. You can also download pictures from:

♦ the internet
♦ an e-mail
♦ a scanner, if your computer is connected to one.
♦ a DVD
♦ or a memory card reader

What's a Memory Card Reader?
They are very handy, small devices that can help you transfer images from your camera to your computer.

A digital camera, without a memory card, only holds about 12 pictures. Memory cards can hold lots of pictures. Think of them like extra rolls of film that you can use over and over again.

There will be a memory card slot somewhere on your camera. Find it, open it, and pop the card out. Sometimes there is a button to push to eject the card, other times you just give the card a little push in and it will pop out.

Slip the card into the reader, then attach the reader into a USB port on your computer.
Now, when you click on File > Import, you will see the reader in the window that opens! Click on the reader icon and then import. Ta Da!

There are as many different sizes and shapes of memory cards as there are cameras. A memory card reader has to be the right size to fit the card....

Now that you've downloaded your pictures...
A little more about the layout of Photo Gallery.

Photo Gallery will open on the Home Tab.

You'll see your picture folders on the left side. Click on a folder to see the pictures inside.

Double click on a picture and you'll see its information on the right column.

Here are the details of what's what along the bottom bar:

Shows how many pictures are in a folder.

Rotate a picture, left or right.

Delete the picture.

View a slide show of all the pictures in the folder.

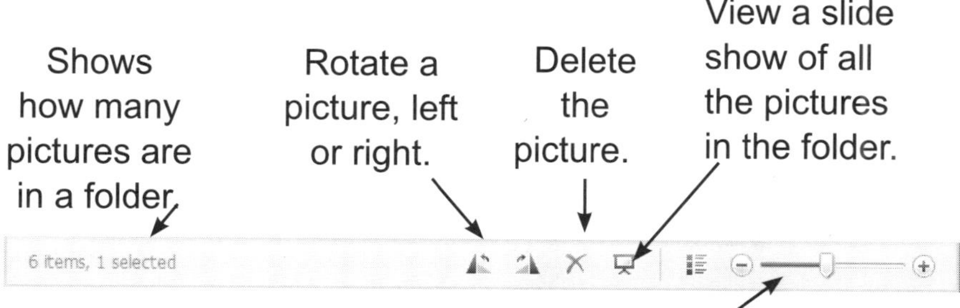

Hold your mouse click down over this slider and move it, to change the size of the pictures you see.

Home tab

Over the next few pages we'll go over what's what under the **Home tab**. I think you are going to like the way things are organized.

We've just gone over how to Import pictures. When you import pictures a new folder is automatically created for them; either as a group or a folder for each date the pictures were taken. Click on **New Folder** to create a folder after the fact.

Why would you want to make a new folder? Think of folders as albums. If you create a new album, you can then grab pictures from any of your other folders to put in it. Wouldn't it be a fun and easy way to make a grow chart for your kids!

Manage
Manage is the next group under the Home tab.
Select all, Copy & Paste, Rotate pictures and *Delete*.

Once you use these, they are easy to remember. So, let's do a quick practice. Everything get's easier with practice!

Let's Practice!!!
New folder, Select All, Copy/Paste, Rotate and Delete.

(All these clicks are left-clicks!)

1. Click your mouse on *Pictures* in the left sidebar.

2. Click on *New Folder* to make a new folder. Leave it named New Folder for this practice.

3. Click on a different folder (album) to see some of your pictures.

4. Click on *Select All* in the Manage group, then *Copy.*

5. Click on the New folder you just created.

6. Click on *Paste*. All the pictures you just copied will arrive.

7. Click on one of the pictures to select it (or you can click on Select All).

8. Click on the top *Rotate* tool to rotate left 90 degrees. Then again for another 90, and again, and again!

9. Click on the other *Rotate* tool to rotate to the right.

10. Since this was all a practice...

11. Click on *Delete*

12. You could have clicked on Select All, then Delete and all the pictures in the folder would be deleted.

If you want to delete the new folder entirely...

1. In the left sidebar, right-click over the new folder to open a mouse menu.

2. Choose Delete

3. A window will open asking you if you are sure you want to do this. Click Yes if you do, No if you don't!

Home > Tags

The next group along the home tab is called **Organize**. It's all about finding your pictures in the future.

Ever have to go rifling through your photo albums looking for some special picture but just can't find it? With the help of the Organizing tools, you'll never lose a picture again! You can:

- ♦ Say who is in the picture
- ♦ Describe it
- ♦ Give it a caption
- ♦ Geotag a picture and say where it was taken
- ♦ Flag it for future reference
- ♦ Even rate it from 1 to 5 stars!

Click on *People tag* and you can say who is in the picture you have selected.

As soon as you click on any of the Organizing tools, the information bar will open on the right side of the window.

You'll see text boxes in the information pane that you can type in. Click your mouse into a text box and type in what you want!

If you Geotag a picture, Photo Gallery will try and confirm that the place is an actual address. *"Mom's rumpus room" won't work.*

Face Recognition

Photo Gallery has
Face Detection AND Face Recognition capability.

Face detection works on most pictures with faces, but not all.
I have no idea why...

When it works, you'll see a thumbnail of their face/s under "Add people tags". And, the faces of the people in the picture will be highlighted, ready for you to tag with an identity.

Face recognition helps with tagging.

After you tag the same person a few times in different pictures, Photo Gallery will start to remember what the person's face looks like, and makes a guess at who it might be by showing a thumbnail picture list of people to choose from.

Photo Gallery is one smart cookie!

Tags

Here's how to add people tags:

1. Open a folder and click on the photo you want to tag.

2. Click on People tag under the Home tab. Photo gallery will look for faces in the picture, and if it finds any you have tagged before, it will offer suggestions in the info pane.

♦   *You can generically tag the picture with names, or you can actually identify people in the picture by left-clicking over their face before you add the tag.*

3. Under People tags in the info pane, start typing a person's name. If the person is one of your Contacts in Mail, their name will show up. Then all you have to do is click on their name to tag them. If they are not one of your contacts, just type in their name.

Now, this is cool!

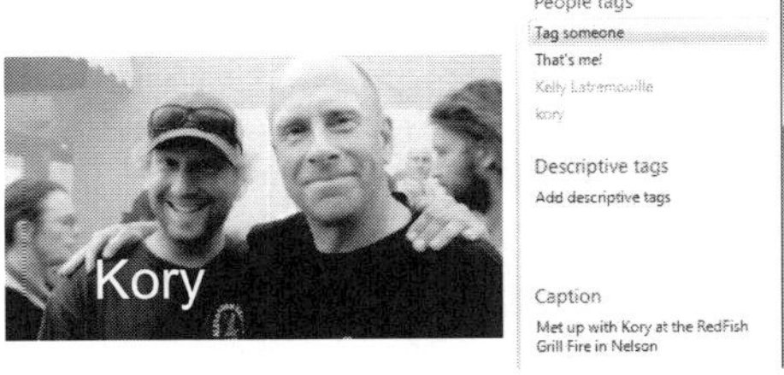

Move your mouse over a picture that you have tagged people in. Their names will now show up when you hover your mouse over their face.

You'll never worry about forgetting who's who again!

If you have tagged your pictures with information, you can use the tools grouped in **Quick find** to find them again. There are more tools for finding pictures under the Find tab.

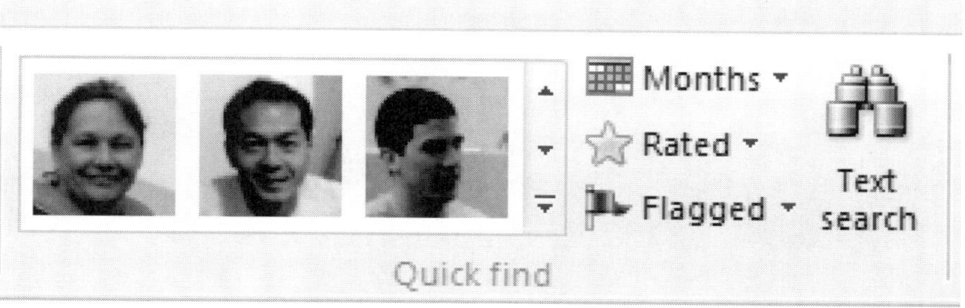

Click on All photos and videos and Photo Gallery will look in all the folders.

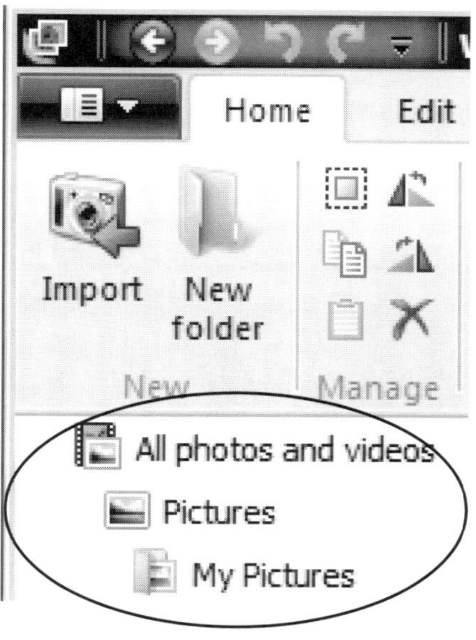

If you have tagged people, their face will show up here with the Quick find tools.
Click on a face in the ribbon, and photos that you've tagged them in will appear in the main window below.

The date, how you rated the picture or if it was flagged are all ways of finding pictures.

Text search is perfect if you have given the picture a description or caption.

No more lost pictures...

Home > Slide show

A slide show is a great way to view your pictures. Click on a folder, then Slide show and off you go.

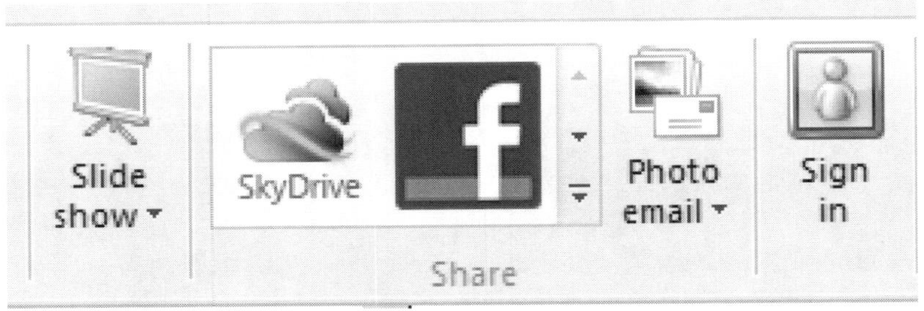

When you watch a slide show, you won't see the Photo Gallery window. The pictures will fill your entire screen.

When the Slide show window opens, **hover your mouse over the top of the screen to see your options.**

You can choose how you would like the pictures to transition by choosing a Theme.

To go back to Photo Gallery's main page, hover your mouse over the top again and click on Back to Photo Gallery when you see it.

Sharing...

**Flikr, Facebook, SkyDrive and YouTube
are social media sites.**

If you are a member of any of these, you can click on the icons to easily upload pictures or videos from your computer.

If you have a Windows Live ID, you have space on SkyDrive. SkyDrive is your *Live* online photo album. Click on a picture or album and then on the *SkyDrive icon* to post the pictures on your SkyDrive. When you post pictures, you can say who can see them; i.e., who you want to *share* them with.
You can also post and share documents on SkyDrive.

This icon is for Windows Live Groups.
You might want to create a Group for your
immediate family, or just you and a friend or some
work colleagues.

When you create a Group you can:

♦ Post pictures that will be seen by that group only.

♦ The group can add or edit pictures.

♦ E-mail everyone at once telling them about the pictures.

♦ Work together and even edit document files.

♦ Coordinate a live Chat using Messenger

To create a Group, click on the Group icon and choose *create a group*. You have to be signed in with your Live ID.

Sharing Safely

SAFETY FIRST

Before you publish a photo to **any on-line** photo gallery, think about what information is on the picture.

Remember that potentially ANYONE who uses the internet can see it. Although by and large most people are good people, not everyone is. *On-line predators are dangerous.*

Really think about how public you want your photos.

There are options on most social media sites where you can say who can see your photos. Get in the habit of using these tools.

Its also a good idea to Google yourself every once in a while. Someone might have tagged you in a photo that you would rather not be shared. For the most part, you can remove personal tags.

Stop. Look. Listen.
Before you cross the street.
Use your eyes and use your ears,
Before you use your feet.

On-line Photo Album Safety Practices

Think about what's in the picture.

- ♦ What's in the background?

- ♦ Do the photos show your house number, license plate, your kids school?

- ♦ Is the photo tagged with full names?

- ♦ Who's in the photo?

- ♦ Will the photo attract the kind of attention you don't want?

- ♦ Will the photo come back and bite you one day? *Employers search Facebook when checking up on potential employees.*

If you have tagged your photos with lots of information, **you can set up Photo Gallery NOT to include any of this information when you publish pictures. Here's how:**

1. Open Photo Gallery

2. Click on the icon to the left of the Home tab to open the menu.

3. Click on Options > Publish

4. Tick *"Remove all file details."*

5. Click OK

Watch where you`re walking
and
Think about what you are posting on the internet.

E-mail Photos

E-mailing pictures from Photo Gallery is a snap!

Here`s how:

1. Click on the picture you want to e-mail.

2. Click on Home > Photo e-mail

3. A new photo e-mail is created with the picture already attatched.

   ♦ If you want to add more pictures, click on *Add more pictures!*

4. Address the e-mail and send.

Tip

Holding down the Shift key (that`s the key that makes capital letters) can help you include more than one picture at a time.

1. Click on a picture to select it.

2. Hold the shift key down.

3. Click on another picture that's a few pictures away.

   ♦ All the the pictures in between the two pictures have now been selected.

Now, when you click on E-mail, all these pictures will be on your photo e-mail!

Want to write down some notes?

Edit Tab

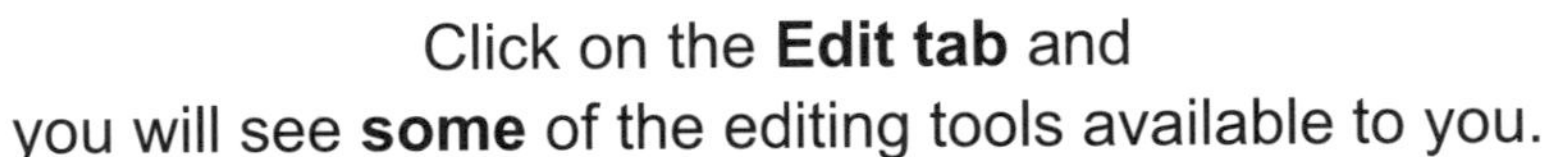

Click on the **Edit tab** and
you will see **some** of the editing tools available to you.

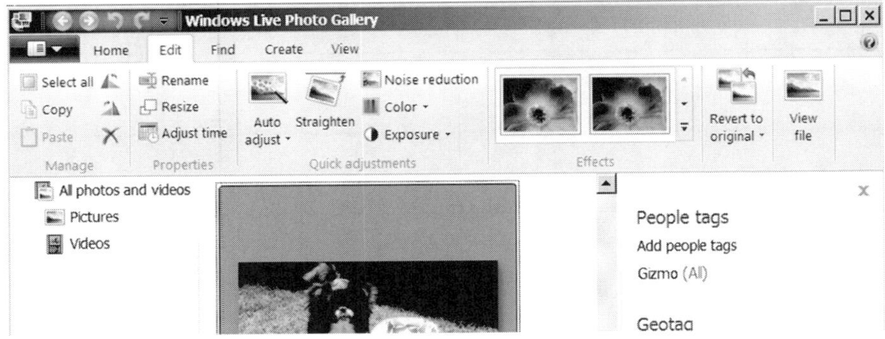

Double click on a picture or click on *View file*
to see **all** of your editing tools.

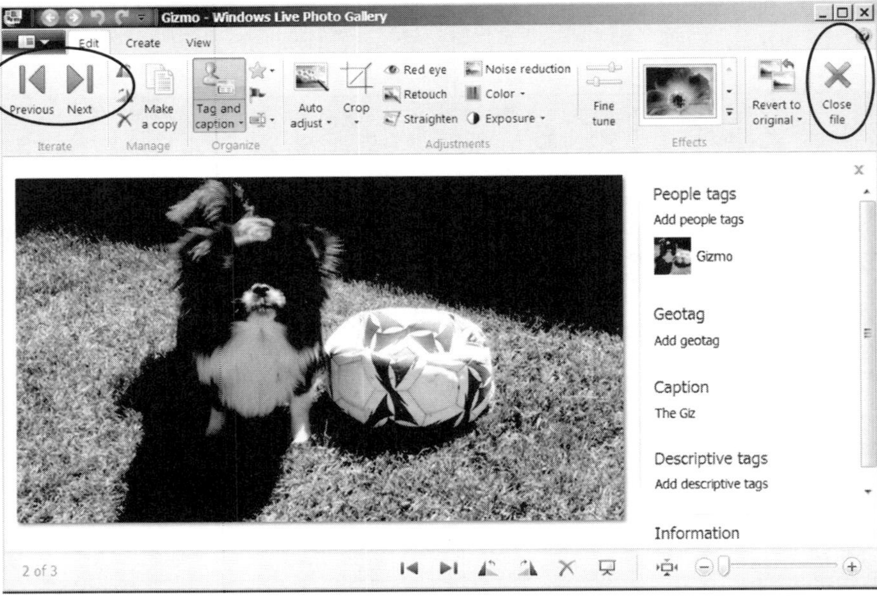

- Use the arrows to scroll through pictures in an album and edit as you go along.
- Click on the X, *Close file*, to save your changes and return to the regular window.

Click on *Fine Tune* to open these tools. Now, click on Adjust exposure to see all you can do with it. Click on the other options to see what you can do with them too.

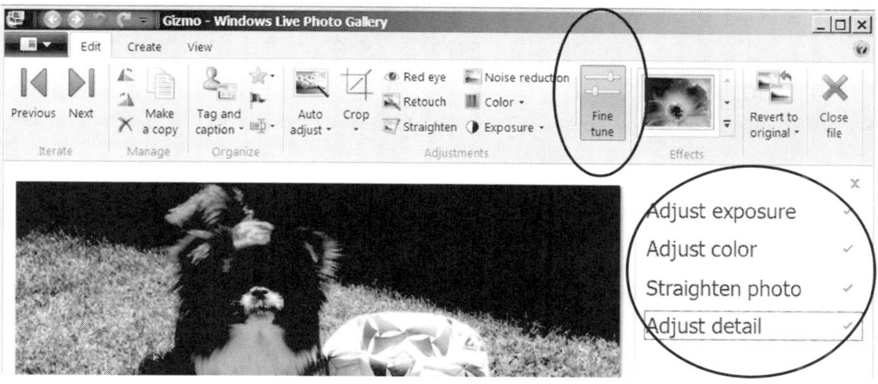

You never have to worry about screwing up a picture by editing it because... Oops, I cropped off Gizmo's head!

- ♦ You can always Undo what you tried, and
- ♦ You can even *Revert to Original* after you save your edits!

These curved arrows are your Undo and Redo tools!

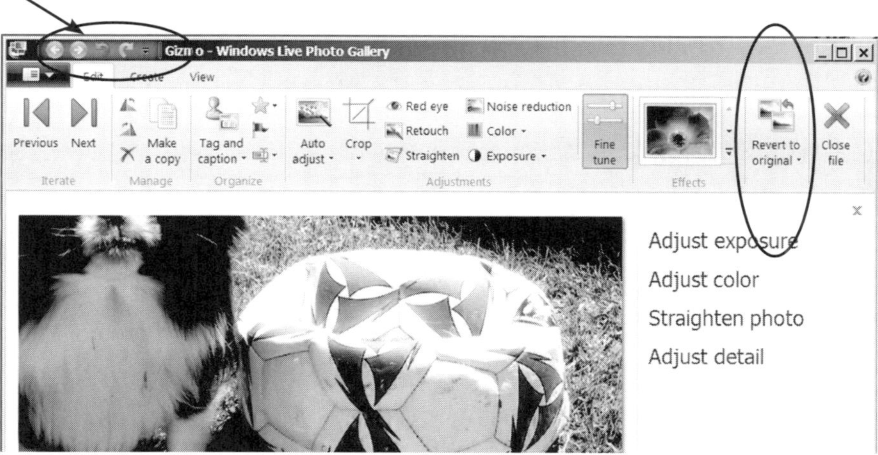

Editing Tools

Here's what the editing tools do:

Auto Adjust

This is the full meal deal option. It will automatically adjust the color and exposure, straighten the photo and try to reduce any noise in the photo. It`s a good tool, but it doesn't always fix the photo the way YOU want it.

Adjust Exposure

You can adjust Brightness, Shadows, Contrast and Highlights. Just use your mouse to move the sliders under each heading to see instant changes.

Adjust Color

Again, it's easy to move the sliders and see your picture change... Lessening the reds, adding a little blue....

Straighten Photo

If your picture is just a little askew, use this to level it out a bit.

Adjust Detail

This helps you "Sharpen" or "Reduce Noise" in an image. Sharpening might help make a blurry picture a little *sharper*. When your picture is grainy, often the case when there is poor lighting, the grainy flecks are referred to as "Noise".

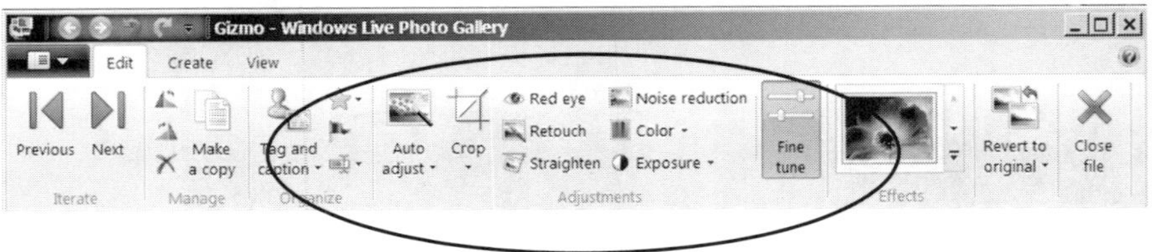

***The editing tools do not work on all image file formats.
They do work on JPG and TIFF formatted files.***

Crop Photo

When you click on Crop Photo, a box, like the one I show here, appears over your picture.

Hold your mouse click down on any of the dots on the box and drag to adjust its size.

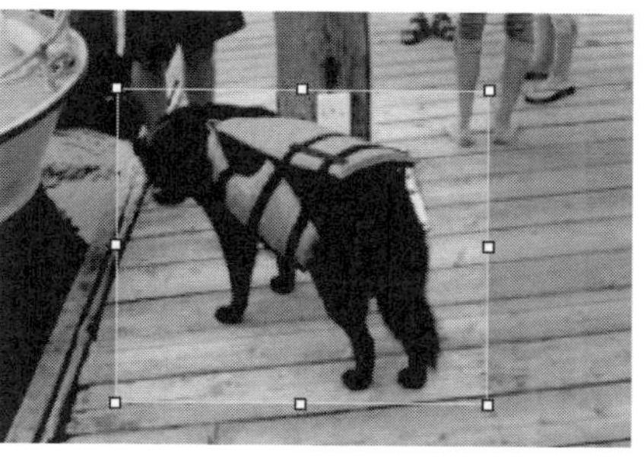

Hold your mouse click down **inside** the box **to move it around** to other parts of your picture. The picture will be cropped to what you see inside the box.

Fix Red Eye

Click on the Red Eye tool, then draw a small box around the eye you want to fix.

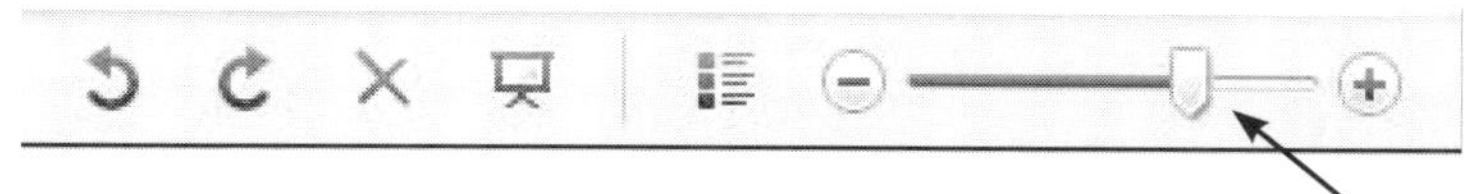

Sometimes it's easier to fix red eye when you are zoomed in closer to the eye. Use the slider to zoom in. If you're having trouble zooming in on an eye, grab the picture, by holding down the left-click on your mouse, and move it.

Effects

You can turn your color photos into black and white and a few other choices here. Take a look, try them out!

Editing Properties

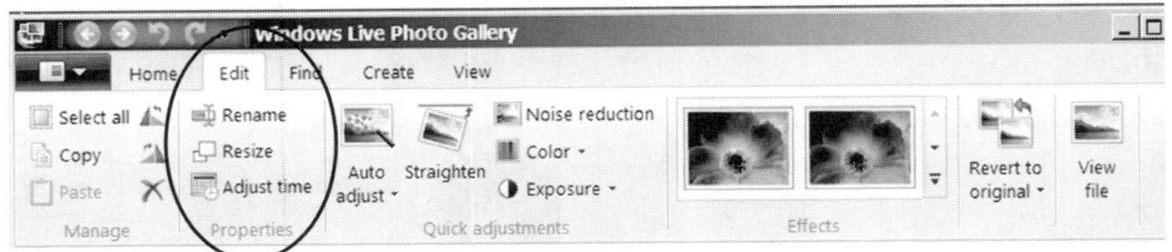

Under the Edit tab...

In the Properties group, Rename and Adjust time don't really need any explaining, but you might wonder about Resize...

Resize

Resizing is different from cropping.

Resizing is about a photo's resolution - how many pixels per inch it has. When you crop a picture, you cut parts of the picture out, keeping only the part you want.

If you want to print a good quality photo, choose a larger *size*. More pixels per inch, gives you higher definition pictures.

If you're only going to view the photo on a computer, choose a size that looks good on your monitor. Often pictures on websites are lower resolution; because they have less data, they will load faster.

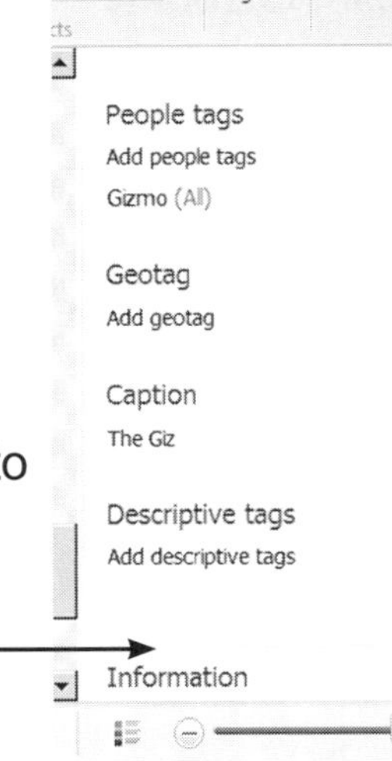

Information

If you rename a picture or adjust the time it was taken,
 you change its *information.*

To expand and see what information a photo has, hover your mouse over the faint line above Information.
Click on the arrow that appears. ⟶

Properties/Information

When you take a picture, your camera automatically saves some information about the picture. It might only be a number, but it could also be the date the picture was taken, what type of camera took the picture, etc. The information that comes from your camera depends on how your camera is programmed.

When you download pictures into Photo Gallery, information from your camera about the pictures will be downloaded too.

You can change, add, delete or update information easily.

Where I show the darker print, you can click your mouse directly there to change or add information.

The info under "Information" is from the camera.

People tags
  Add people tags
  That`s me!

Descriptive tags
  Add descriptive tags

Caption
  Add caption

Information
Filename: IMG.0123.JPG
Date taken   18/05/2010
                 9:36 AM
Size   2.13 MB
Dimensions   33264 x 2338
Rating   👍👍👍👍👍
Camera   Canon
Author   Add an author
Exposure   1/60 sec
Aperture   f/2.6
Focal length   5.8 mm
ISO   400

Print Pictures.

Funny that there isn't a nice big icon for regular old printing at home. Maybe they'll add it in an update someday. In the meantime...

Here's how to print pictures with your printer!

1. First, select a picture to print (by clicking on it).

2. Then **click on the little icon that's left of Home, to open Photo Gallery's menu.**

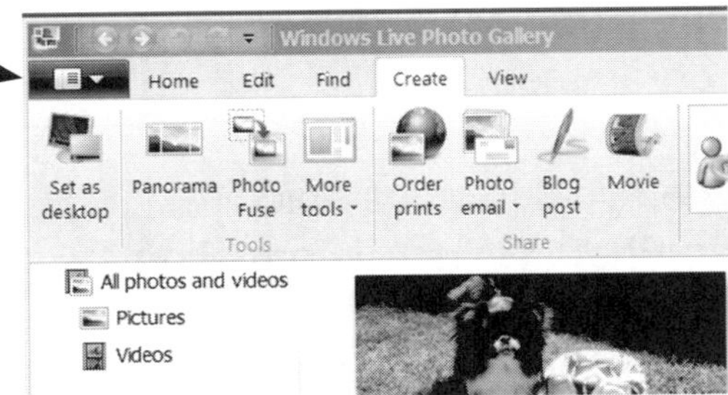

3. Click on Print when you see it in the menu.

4. You will open the print window with all your options.

♦ See the little arrows below where it says Printer, Paper size, Quality and Paper type. Click on the arrows to open your choices.

♦ If you want your pictures to look like they've come from the photo shop, use actual photo paper in your printer.

♦ Click your mouse on the different layout options, seen in the right column. *Especially if you don't want to print a big 8 x 10!*

♦ How many copies do you want?

5. Click on Print when you are ready.

Remember about picture "size"?
If you want to print a clear crisp picture, you are going to want to make sure it has a high pixel count. Edit tab > Resize...

Want to make some notes?

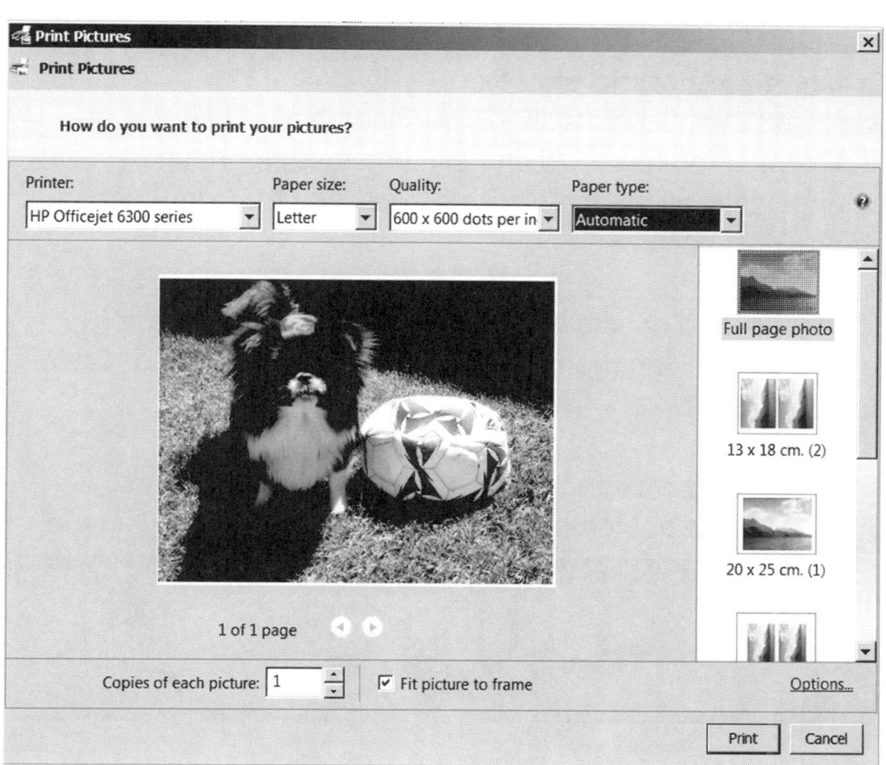

Create Tab > Panorama

Get Creative!

It's nice to have a favorite picture for your desktop background.

Click on a picture to select it, then use this tool to make it your desktop background.

Panorama and
Photo fuse are very cool tools! What makes them even better is that they are easy to use. Here's what's what.

Create a panoramic photo...
Really quite amazing technology. It combines a series of pictures that you have and *stitches* them together! It automatically aligns the pictures and turns them into one photo.

All you have to do is select the photos you want to *stitch* together by ticking them, then click **Panorama**. Photo Gallery does all the work.

Here's a picture stitch of our backyard garden.
Imagine the photo you could create of the Grand Canyon!

Photo Fuse

Now you have another good reason for using the rapid fire on your camera. You know how hard it is to take a good family portrait.

Photo Fuse can help you make everyone look good!

Here's what's what with Photo Fuse:

This is the best of the bunch of family portraits you took, but Grandma's got her eyes closed.

In one of your other pictures, Grandma looks great. If only you could replace Grandma's good face picture with the bad one. With Photo Fuse, you can!

Here's how:

♦ Select both pictures by ticking them.
♦ Click on Photo fuse
   Photo gallery composites the two pictures, looking for the similarities.
♦ In the new window that opens, you'll see a "crop box" on one picture and thumbnails of both pictures you selected on the side.
♦ You can adjust the size of the crop box and move it around on the photo till it is showing just what you want to exchange.
♦ Then pick the best version of the picture from what you're shown in the thumbnails.
♦ Click on Save.
♦ You'll save a new version of the two pictures. You won't delete or change the originals.

More Tools...

Download more photo tools..

This is a funky way that Microsoft has enabled quick links to new tools that are being developed for Photo Gallery.
If you`re feeling ready to expand your horizons click on this and see what`s in store for you!

Be adventurous... Click on More tools.
You just might find something
that's just your cup-a-tea!

Next along the ribbon is *Order Prints*...

Order prints works if Microsoft has set up a partnership with someone in your area for this service.

That's not the case for me. So sorry, I can't help you out with this. Instead, I'll talk about sending your photos out to a location of your choice. **How to manually order prints!**

Manually Order Prints

If your local drug or grocery store as a photo department, ask them if they offer online service as well. Many small independent photo shops offer online photo service too.

You can order prints from most of the big chains like Walmart or Costco. All you have to do is register with them online, then upload the pictures you want to print.

Photo upload sites are generally set up very well and are easy to use. And, the service is FAST. Here's a story to prove it...

My story about ordering prints online.

After we got home from holidays last summer I thought my Mom would like copies of some of the pictures we took.

I knew the Walmart in Nelson had a photo department so I logged onto Walmart's website and clicked on Photos.
I registered with my name and put Mom's name as the person who was picking up, along with her phone number. Then I chose the location of the store where I wanted the pictures to be picked up.

I clicked on Next and browsed through the pictures on my computer that I wanted to send Mom. Then I had the option to pay at pick up or, pay now (I paid for them...) That was it.

I thought I better e-mail Mom and let her know I was sending her some pictures. As I was typing the e-mail she phoned me — Walmart just called saying there were pictures there for her! It wasn't 10 minutes since I sent them.
Now that's FAST!
She was as impressed as I was. Good professionally printed pictures in a heartbeat sent from miles away.
Gotta love that.

Create > Blog Post

Photo e-mail is next along the ribbon, but, as Photo e-mail is also under the Home tab, we've already learned about it!! Next, Blog Post.

What's a Blog? Why a web log, of course...

Blogging is akin to an online diary, with a difference. Blogs are meant to be public and interactive, often allowing visitors to leave comments or even send the blogger a message.

Blog post works together with *Windows Live Writer,* Microsoft's blogging program. *Writer* is part of the Windows Live Essentials suite of programs.
When you click on *Blog post,* Writer opens.
Remember for the tools to be active, you have to select a picture first

When you use Writer for the first time, you will have to let it know where you want your blog published.

Microsoft recently partnered with WordPress.com who will now host bloggers with Live ID's for free.

When Writer opens, the first thing you should do is set up your blog account. You have to tell Writer where you want to publish your blog. ***Find "Add an Account" by clicking here.***

From Blog Post to Writer

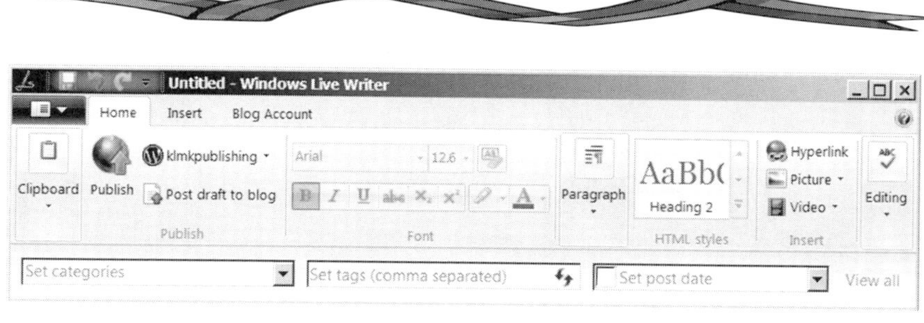

I'm not going to get much more into using Writer or blogging. If you are keen on blogging, you will find Writer is an easy program to use. You can use almost any blogging host/server, *not just WordPress.com.*

But I will help you with what a couple things mean when you're setting up an account.

> If you set up with WordPress.com your blog name will become part of your blog address, for example:

♦ If the *blog name* is KLMKPublishing.

♦ The *blog address* is http://klmkpublishing.wordpress.com

♦ The *remote hosting server* is the same as the *blog address.*

If you are new to blogging, check out some blogs to see what they are about. I'm blown away by some of the adventures I read about.

For instance, James and Lorna Wilding are sailing around the world, their blog posts are inspiring, their photography, beautiful.

Check them out if you like, the address is: http://my.opera.com/cjwilding/blog/

Create > Movie...

Next along the ribbon is *Movie.*
When you click on *Movie,* the program
Windows Live Movie Maker opens.

 *Movie Maker* is part of the Windows Live Essentials suite of programs. If you haven't downloaded it and you'd like to use this tool, download it now.

Movie Maker can turn your snaps
into a slide show with panache.

Here's how:

1. Select the pictures you want to include in the "movie" by ticking them.

2. Click through Create > Movie

3. **Windows Live Movie Maker will open.**

If you want to create a slide show with music or sound,
Movie Maker is the program to use.

Movie Maker

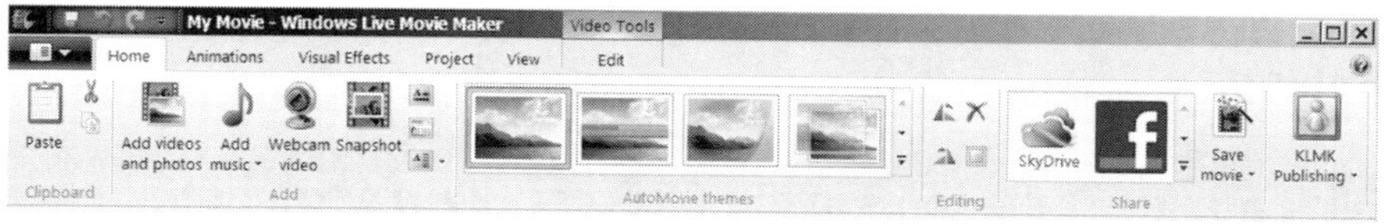

Within Movie Maker you'll find the tools for fancying up a slide show. Like adding music, including captions, colorizing, etc. Movie Maker is very well laid out and straightforward to use.

When Movie Maker opens you will see all the photos you selected there, ready for you to work with. Try out all the options, play with things.

The best way to learn here is to use it.
Go ahead, you're going to have fun!

Movie Maker loves to Share too!
Click on the icons in the Share group to easily upload the movie to any of the social media sites, maybe YouTube. (You have to register as a user on YouTube to use YouTube.)

Save your movies.
Click on Save Movie (on the right side of the ribbon) to see your options. Do you have a CD/DVD Burner as part of your computer? This is where the tools are to save your movies onto DVDs.

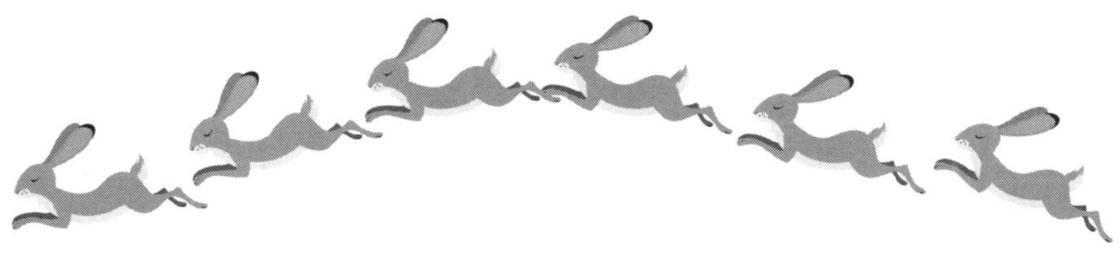

View Tab

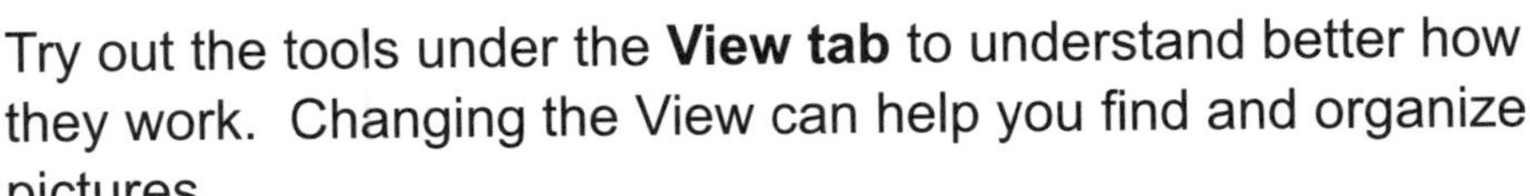

Try out the tools under the **View tab** to understand better how they work. Changing the View can help you find and organize pictures.

Click on any of the tools in the first group, ***Arrange list,*** and your pictures will re-sort themselves into the various categories. Date, Person, Geotag, Name, Published...

Click on any of the tools in the second group, ***Show details***, to see the details beside each individual picture.

Zoom-in and Zoom-out are the next tools along the ribbon. Use these tools, if you don't like using the slider at the bottom of the window for enlarging and shrinking the view of the pictures on your screen.

Slide show is such a popular tool, it's here under View too!

Tag and Caption Pane. Click on this tool and a third column will open showing the information a picture has. Having this column in view is an easy way to add captions and tags.

Bits and Bytes

The next few pages are a bit of a mixed bag. You'll find answers to some of my most common questions. From deleting files to enabling European keys.

If you find yourself stuck on something, don't hesitate to send me your question. I'm happy to try and help you out.

Louise@MyParentsFirst.com

Bits and Bytes

You might find that it's easy to create files by mistake; I know I do. Don't worry though, it's easy to delete unwanted files. **Here's how:**

Open Windows Explorer, by clicking on the Windows Explorer icon in your taskbar. (Not to be confused with the Internet Explorer icon.) This icon looks like a file folder.

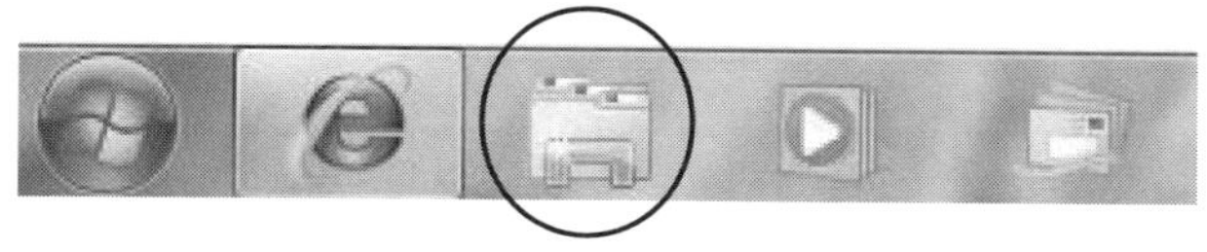

In the Windows Explorer window you will see Libraries in the left column, and its folders listed under it: Documents, Pictures, Music, etc. Click on a folder to view its contents.

Remember how you can change how you view your files? Click on this icon and choose details or thumbnails.

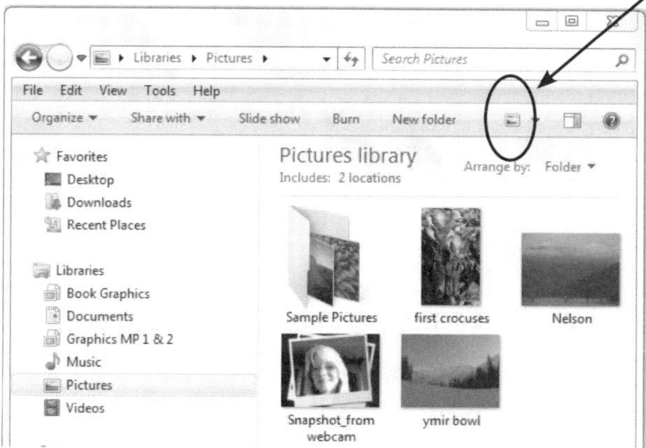

Here's how to delete a file:

♦ Click on the file to select it, then press the d

♦ elete key on your keyboard. Or,

♦ Right click over a file to open a mouse menu, then slide your mouse up to Delete and left click.

Recycle Bin

Your computer has a Recycle Bin, it's where files go when you delete them. You'll see an icon for it on your desktop.

How to open the Recycle Bin
To open the Recycle Bin, either double-click on its icon or, left-click over the icon to open a mouse menu, then click on Open.

When your Recycling folder is open, it will show all the files and folders that you have deleted since the last time it was emptied. This is a good thing, because if you deleted something by mistake, at this point it's easy to get it back.

How to retrieve files from the Recycle Bin

1. Open the Recycle bin.

2. Click on the file you want to retrieve.

3. Up on the toolbar, click on "Restore this item". *Did you notice that before you clicked on a file, "Restore this item" said "Restore all items".*

    Zoom — back it goes to its original folder!

You can also drag files from the Recycle Bin and drop them into folders within your Library or onto your Desktop. *How to drag and drop is just over the page!*

The Recycle Bin is your safety net!

It is also important to Empty the Recycle Bin!

When you are sure that there is NOTHING in the Recycle bin that you want to retrieve, empty it.

Here's how to Empty the Recycle bin:
1. Click on the Recycle Bin icon to open it.
2. On the toolbar, click on "Empty the Recycle Bin"

Once you have emptied the Recycle Bin,
files are gone forever... *Unless you are a tech wizard!*

Tip:

Did you accidentally delete the Recycle Bin from your desktop?

1. Right-click anywhere on your desktop to open a mouse menu.

2. Click on "Personalize".

3. In the left sidebar of the window that opened, click on "Change desktop icons".

You'll be able to restore it from here!

Moving files

Drag and drop to move files!
It's all too easy to save a file in the wrong folder.
But no worries, files are easy to move!
Here's how:

1. Open Windows Explorer by clicking on its icon on the taskbar.

2. If you know where the file you want to move is, click on that folder to open it. If you don't know, type the name of the file in the Windows Explorer's search window.

3. Now that you can see the file you want, HOLD your mouse left-click down over it.

4. Keep holding down the left-click and DRAG the file to the folder you want it in.

5. When you see the folder you want the file moved to highlight itself, let go of the mouse click to DROP the file.

That's it!

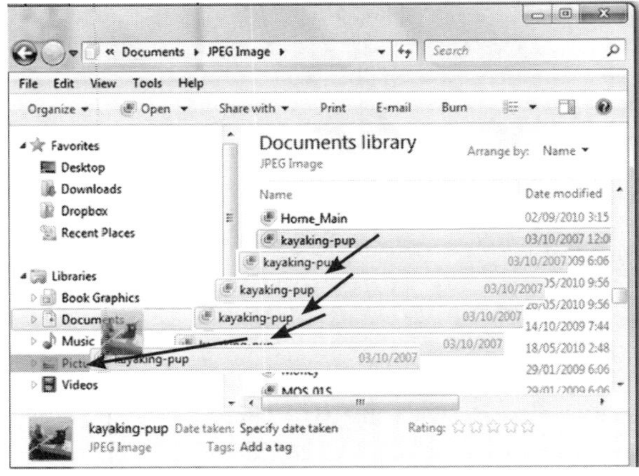

Browsing for Files

Here are a couple of reasons you might find yourself browsing for files to upload onto a website:

♦   To upload a picture of an item to sell on eBay.

♦   To upload a new profile picture of yourself for Facebook.

When a website offers the option to browse for and upload files from your computer, you will see a window like this:

When you click on "Browse", your Windows Explorer folder will open so you can browse for the picture or file you want.

Here, under Libraries, I clicked on Pictures to open the Pictures folder.

When I saw the picture I wanted, I clicked over it.

The file name will show up in the "File Name" box.

Click on "Open" and the file will start uploading.

When you return to the Browse window, along with the name of the file, you will see the "path" that the website will use to find the file in your computer.

You'll probably see an OK button near the Browse window. Click on OK and your file will upload to the site.

The Control Panel

The Control Panel is where you can adjust the settings on your computer, including: adjusting the time and creating a home or office network.

It's also where you go to Uninstall a program that you don't want any more. (Never delete a program directly from the Start menu, use Uninstall instead).

To open the Control Panel, click on the Start button. Start > Control Panel

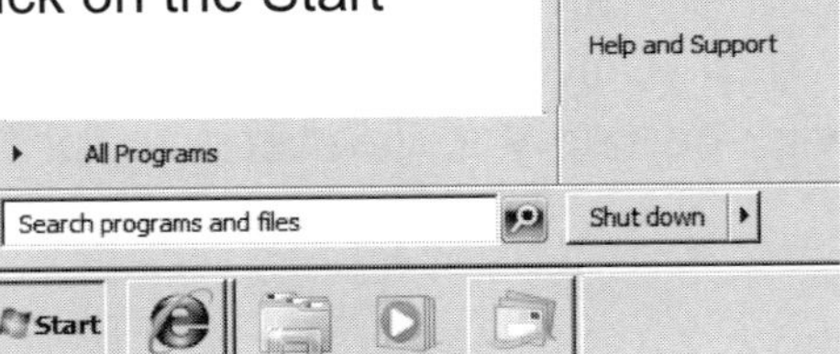

The "View" of the Control Panel I show here is by "Icons". I like this view because it shows me everything listed. The other *view* is by Category, where things are grouped together.

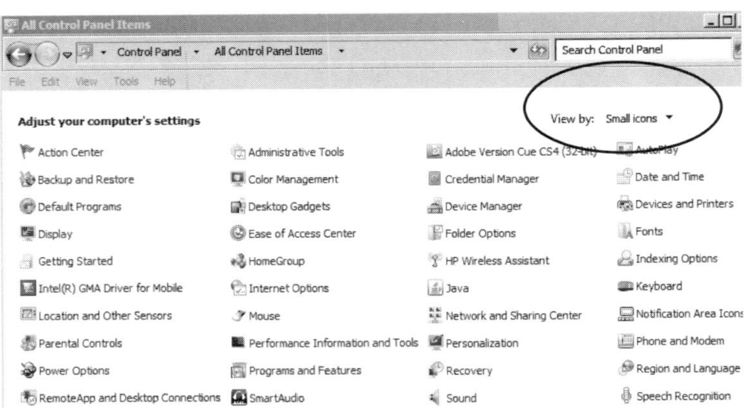

Have a look around in here, but don't mess with things you are not sure about — like changing your hardware or driver settings. *Look to the next page for things you can mess with!*

The Control Panel

Within the Control Panel you can adjust or customize many things. Here are just a few:

◊   Customize your Desktop.

◊   Adjust your Keyboard settings.

◊   Set the Parental Controls.

◊   Program scheduled tasks, such as defragging!

◊   Set your Power Saving options.

◊   Set how your mouse works.

◊   Adjust the date and time — even the time zone!

Add a Printer

You can open the Printer and Devices window from the Control Panel or directly from the Start menu.
Start > Printers and Devices.

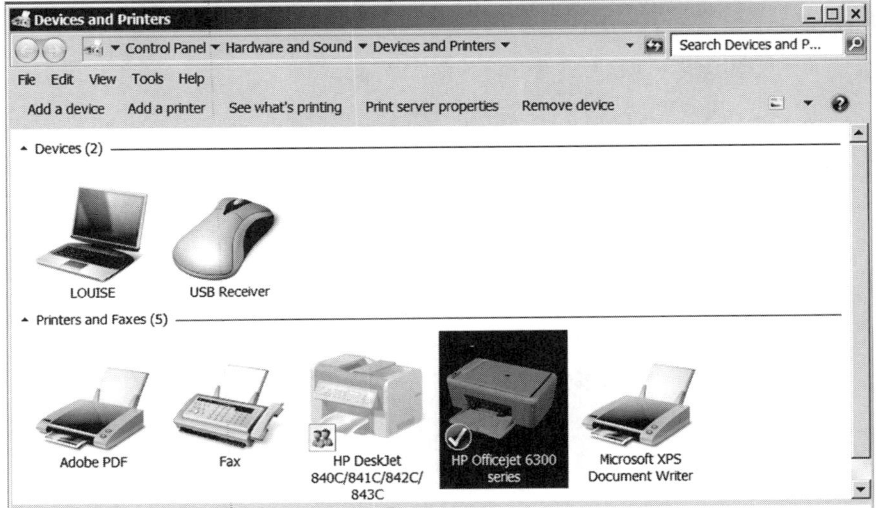

This is what's in my computer, yours will be different.

Under **Devices** it shows my laptop and wireless mouse.

Under **Printers and Faxes**, can you see the check mark by the HP Officejet? (In real life its green.) The check mark tells me that this is the printer that my computer will look to use, it's the *default* printer.

When you connect your computer to a new printer with a USB connection, Windows 7 will automatically do the installation.

After a printer is installed, you will see an icon for it in this window. If the green check mark is not on it, right-click over the printer's icon and choose "make default". That's it!

There are lots of reasons you might want to adjust your printer settings. Here are just a few:

♦ You might want to change the print quality from Draft quality for everyday printing, to Photo quality for printing pictures.

♦ You might want to change the orientation from Landscape to Portrait.

♦ You might be using a different size of paper or print on an envelope.

You can adjust your printer settings from the Printer Settings window. **Right-click** over the printer's icon to open a menu, then **left-click** on **Printing Preferences.**

You will open a window similar to this one where you can adjust the settings.

Click on each of the drop-down arrows and the tabs to see your options.

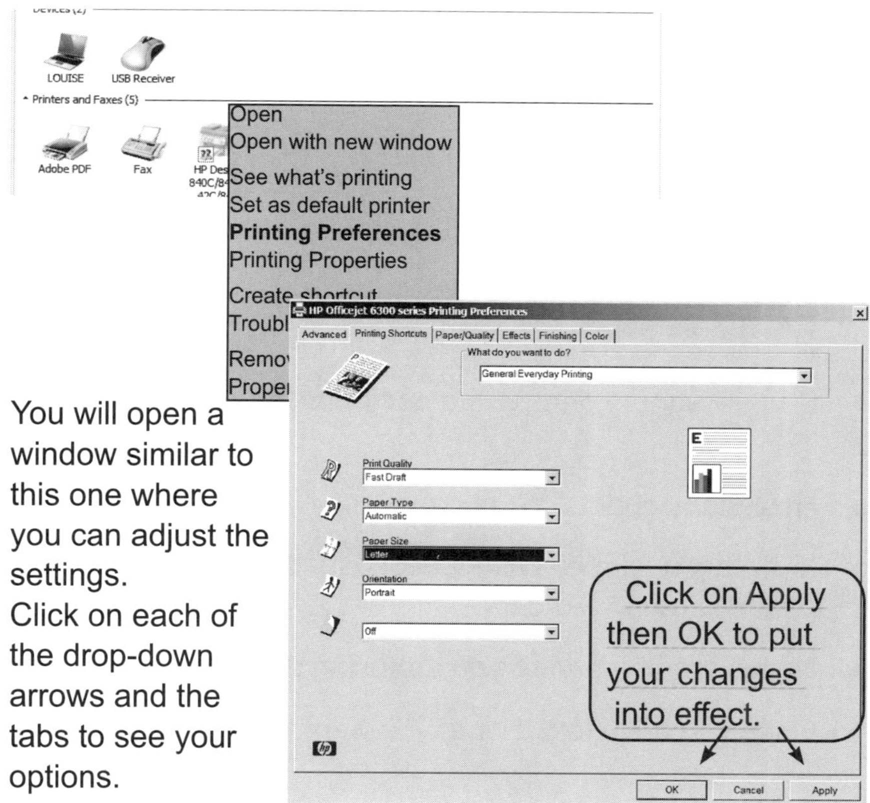

Printing

The Print command in many programs is found in the File menu along a Menu bar. In the Live Essentials programs, **you'll find the Print command by clicking on the little icon left of the Home tab.** In the menu that opens click on Print.

Once you click on Print, a window similar to this one will open where you can tell it what you want to do.

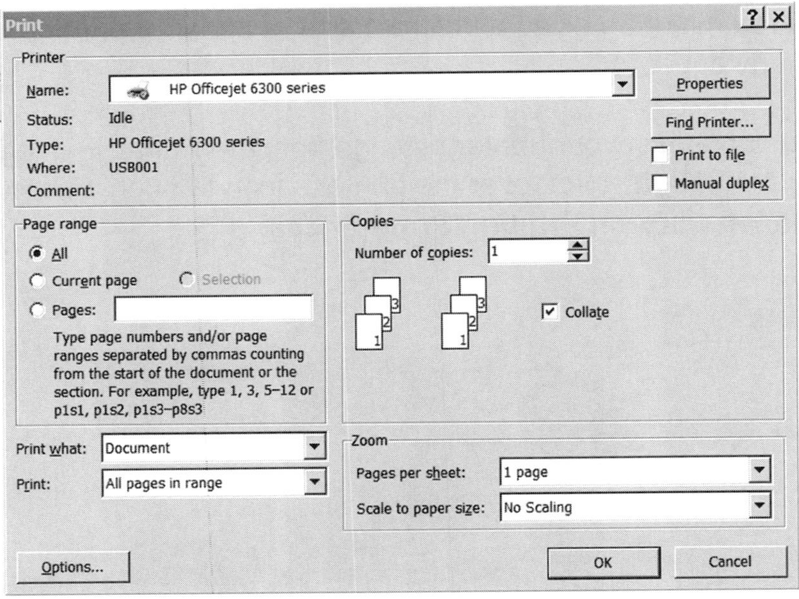

- Do you want to print all the document or just a selection of it?

- How many copies do you want?

- Is it a big document with lots of pages? Do you want it to print it in reverse order?

- Notice that the printer you are using is in the "Name' box.

- Once you have told it what you want, click on OK to print.

Ejecting Media

Have a look at the icons on the right side of your taskbar.

The icons on your computer will probably be a little different than what I show here. If you hover your mouse over the icons your computer, you'll see their name appear!

Safely Remove Hardware and Eject Media icon

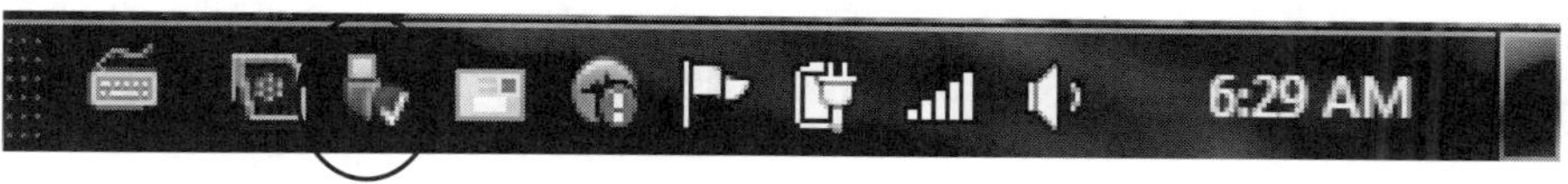

If you connect an mp3 player (iPod), camera, smart phone...,
anything, to your computer
this icon will show up in your
taskbar. **Here's how to use it:**

♦ Click on this icon and you
  will see the option to Eject
  the media.

♦ Click on Eject and it will tell
  you if its safe to remove
  the device or, if you have to
  close or turn off something first.

Telling your computer that you are going to disconnect or eject media that is attached to your computer is an important safety step. By doing this you will help keep the integrity of the files that are within your media or device.

Many programs have an *eject media* command. Photo Gallery has one so you can disconnect your camera safely, as does iTunes, so you can safely disconnect your iPod.

European Key Snafu

Some keyboards have extra symbols on the keys. Nice to have, but frustrating if you accidentally activate the keys. I can't tell you how many times I've done that. All of a sudden instead of typing a question mark I'm getting É instead.

On my keyboard, the European key symbols are marked in blue. Your keyboard may or may not have this feature.

Here's how to turn On and Off the European keys:

To turn them On:
- Press these keys at the same time:
  The Ctrl key + the Left-shift key + the Right-Shift key
- Let go of the keys and try your keyboard to see if it worked.

To turn them Off:
- Press these keys at the same time:
  The Ctrl key + the Left-shift key + the Right-Shift key
- Then while still holding down the Ctrl and Left-shift keys, release the Right-Shift key, then press it down again.
- Let go of the keys and try your keyboard to see if it worked.

You might also try and see what results you get if you replace the Ctrl key with either the fn or Alt keys. Figuring just what combination will work can be a bit of a snafu!

Frozen Computer

It's happened to all of us... all of a sudden the computer freezes and becomes totally unresponsive. Could be any number or reasons why, maybe just too many things to think about at one time. More important though, is being able to get it going again!
Here a couple of ways to re-start a frozen computer.

First, try this key combination to re-start your computer:

Hold these keys down at the same time:
♦   CTRL + Alt + Delete
♦   Let go, then press them again. CTRL + Alt + Delete

If that doesn't work, you might have to "cold boot" your computer. Here's how:

♦   Turn it off by using the power button. On a desktop computer, the power button is on the CPU.
♦   You may have to hold the power button down for up to 10 seconds for it to turn off.
♦   Let the computer rest for at least 30 seconds.
♦   Press the power button again to turn it on.

When the computer comes back on, it might want to run a diagnostic and try to recover what you were working on. Let it do its thing!

Gadgets

Put some fun on your desktop with Gadgets.

Gadgets are wee little programs that run on your desktop.

There are gadgets that show you the weather, gadgets that tell you the time, calendars, ones that show you the headlines. There are hundreds of them, for all sorts of things!

A few gadgets are probably already installed on your computer. **To see what's in yours**, right-click on your desktop to open the desktop mouse menu, then click on Gadgets.

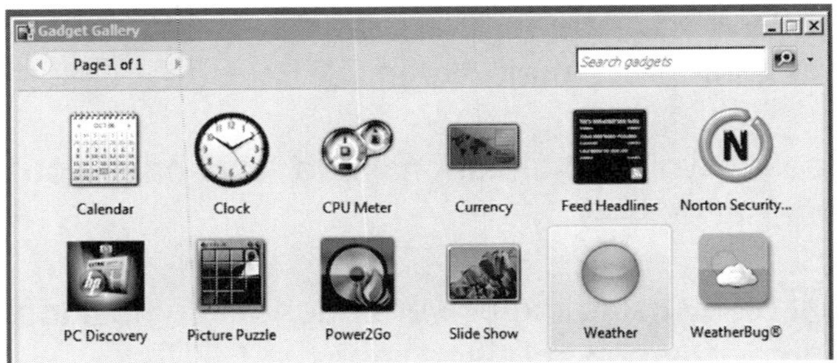

Right-click over a gadget to add it to your desktop.

Hover your mouse over a gadget on your desktop and you'll see its options.

- Exit or Close
- Change its size
- The gadget's options
- Hold your mouse click down on this to move it.

You can find all sorts of gadgets on the Microsoft website. You'll see a link to the site on the gadget window. "Get more gadgets online"!

Snap, Peek and Shake!

You can move windows around on your screen.
Here's how:

1. Move your mouse up to the menu bar at the top of a window.

2. Click and hold down the left-click on your mouse.

3. Holding down the click, you can now drag the window around on your screen.

4. Let go of the mouse-click to drop the window where you want it.

SNAP!

With Snap you can drag a window off to the side or top of your screen and it will automatically re-size itself to fill half of the screen. This is a nice feature for comparing windows!

PEEK

Peek is a feature of Windows 7, found on the very right side of your taskbar. Click on that small blurry square to expose your desktop.
Everything open will get reduced to icons on your taskbar.

SHAKE

Shake is a Windows 7 feature that helps un-clutter your desktop of open windows. Hold your mouse click down over the menu bar on an open window and give it a shake. All the windows except that one you're holding disappears. Shake the window again and — Voila!— they are back again!

Time to Play

Most computers come with a ton of games.

Open the Start menu and type "Games" in the search window to see what's in yours!

Make time to play.

It's good for you!

Write down your own bright ideas!

Bright Ideas

Write down your own bright ideas!

Index

Index

Index

Index

Live, Love, Learn

My Dad was diagnosed with lung cancer in 2001 and passed away from the disease in 2003. He never lost hope; he never gave up. Through it all, he continued to go at life with a positive attitude.

Back then, my family and I were living on the East Coast and my parents were in the West. I was frustrated by the distance between us, feeling like there was nothing I could do.

Before the cancer, Mom and Dad never wanted a computer. They had just, finally, got an answering machine! But they saw how useful the internet was to get information, and how much easier communication would be with e-mail. So, when my brother gave them his old computer, they relented and tried to figure out how to use it.

Finally, I could help with something! I started sending them notes, teaching them how to use their new computer.

Dad loved it. When he got too sick to go to Bridge Club, he could play bridge on the computer. And Mom surfs around like a pro now.

I will forever be inspired by their resilience.

I wish for you the joy of learning too.

- Louise